DUST THOU ART

Finding God, Happiness,
and Fulfillment

Captain R. Stewart Fisher, USN, Ret.

SIGNALMAN PUBLISHING

Dust Thou Art
Finding God, Happiness, and Fulfillment
by R. Stewart Fisher

Signalman Publishing
www.signalmanpublishing.com
email: info@signalmanpublishing.com
Kissimmee, Florida

ISBN: 978-1-940145-28-0 (paperback)
978-1-940145-29-7 (ebook)

Library of Congress Control Number: 2014944670

Printed in the United States of America

SIGNALMAN
PUBLISHING

*Dedicated to our loving God, family, children,
grandchildren, and future generations.*

Contents

Foreword
from Coach John Wooden

Captain Stew Fisher's third book, *Dust Thou Art: Finding God, Happiness, and Fulfillment*, is another outstanding effort and a great companion to his first two books: *Inspiring Leadership: Character and Ethics Matter* and *Leave a Legacy: Reflections on the Strategies of Great Leadership*.

In his latest book, Stew explores the soul-searching questions man has asked since he first walked upright and goes on to examine his relationship to a loving God. It is a deep and insightful look at what it means to be human and why we are here.

He reminds us that there is a wonderful purpose for our existence, but it cannot be fulfilled without a strong connection to Almighty God. Disconnected from Him, "we are nothing more than dust." But in concert with Him, we can achieve the greatness He intended for each of us.

To be sure, we often stumble. We can be weak, proud, arrogant, cruel, lazy, and unfeeling. But we can also be generous, strong, selfless, creative, kind, and loving. We only rise to our best selves when we seek God's help. Apart from Him, we are nothing.

Stew tells us that great leaders spend their entire lifetimes working on self-improvement. They certainly can't lead others until they have mastered themselves. They lead by example and adhere to the highest standards of conduct. But without the help of a loving God, this lifelong quest for self-improvement and inspiring leadership is destined to fail. If we begin to think that we can do it on our own, we're sadly mistaken, and we quickly lose our way. Stew also reminds us that God seldom shouts at us, but rather talks in a whisper to the depths of our souls.

Stew points out that inspiring leaders see mistakes for what they really are: wonderful opportunities for growth and learning. In fact, obstacles and setbacks are often sent to us as part of God's plan for our own self-improvement. Great leaders understand that "calm seas do not make good sailors" and that success is often the last event in a long line of failures. They realize that they themselves are certainly not perfect, so why should they hold others to an impossible standard.

They seek *excellence*, but not *perfection*. All that really matters is that everyone has done his best. True leaders inspire their teams by telling them that *they will cherish and share for a lifetime the memories of great achievement, but that mediocrity never leads to fulfillment and is quickly forgotten.*

In *Dust Thou Art* Stew tells us that inspiring leaders seek balance in their own lives and for the people they lead. They constantly work to enhance body, mind, and spirit, knowing these are the three pillars for a fulfilling life. They are fun to be around and are able to laugh easily at their own human foibles. They are able to "age gracefully" with their sights set on a greater prize beyond mere earthly existence.

Stew has written another marvelous book that captures what it means to be human and our relationship to Almighty God. It resonates with the themes in my own books, especially *Wooden: A Lifetime of Reflections On and Off the Court*. The principles Stew and I both learned in the Navy reaffirm those that my dad, Joshua Wooden, taught me so many years ago on our Indiana farm. They apply in both military and civilian life, in all ages, and across all cultures.

Dust Thou Art is a timeless and wonderful book that you will want to keep on the shelf and refer to often. It explores the very same principles I used in my long coaching career at UCLA, and more importantly, as a father and a husband. It's another great read!

Acknowledgments

I always admired UCLA Coach John Wooden for his strength of character and strong moral leadership. In a conversation I had with him before he died, I discovered that we shared a mutual admiration for many of the same leaders: the Good Lord, Abraham Lincoln, Mother Teresa, Martin Luther King, John F. Kennedy, and Robert E. Lee.

Coach Wooden graciously agreed to write the foreword for my book, and for that I am eternally grateful. We encounter leaders like Coach Wooden once in a generation. To share time with him was a rare privilege and one I'll never forget. I knew I was in the presence of greatness.

John Donne was so right when he said, "No man is an island." We are all touched by many people in our lives. My only fear is that I might leave someone out who truly deserves to be mentioned.

It should come as no surprise that I thank Audrey and Robert Fisher, my mom and dad, and Dr. John Fisher and Marian Kunz, my brother and sister, for their love and encouragement over all these years. My mom was an "Irish tiger" when it came to defending her kids.

My Godmother, Aunt Ruth Macdonald, always kept me going with her words of encouragement. She's still an inspiration to me today, even though she passed away recently at age 100.

My uncle, Ben Ashcraft, was a great role model. Whenever he would see me beating myself up over some mistake I had made, he would simply ask, "Well, did you learn something?" He made me realize that was all that really mattered in life: learning from our mistakes and moving on.

My cousins, Phil and Tinki Kilkeary, provided a welcome "port in a storm" during my days at Annapolis. They had a home just up the Severn River from the Academy and generously let me use their sailboat during June Week.

I also benefited from my grandparents' wisdom, and spent many hours listening to them over cups of coffee at the kitchen table. Later, when my granddad died, Norm Johanning filled that role and mentored me over many summers on Grand Traverse Bay in northern Michigan. I tagged along with him so much that he nicknamed me "Friday."

And who can forget those remarkable nuns at Sacred Heart Grade School and Saint Patrick's High who kept us on the "straight and narrow": Sisters Donata, Alicia, Jerom, Leonita, Marie Agatha, Marie Ouelette, and Paraclita. How they put up with us all those years I'll never know.

At the Naval Academy, I was blessed with many great friends: Colonel Hank and Beverly Richard, Captain Hendrix, Ron and Anne Spratt, Jim and Dianne Theis, Perry Martini, Mike Delbalzo, Bruce Gallemore, Garry Holmstrom, Craig Welling, Jim

Barron, Mark Horgan, Bill Hall, and Ross Dessert, to name just a few.

During the course of my career in the Navy, I served with many fine officers and sailors whose influence is felt to this day: Mac McLaughlin, Gene Pellerin, Steve Arends, Maury Docton, Lindsay Blanton, Chuck Erickson, Rick Haupt, Ray Hann, Dick Thomson, Gary Glashauser, Steve Keith, Dave Johnson, Bob Peyton, Bob Brockmeier, George Kokkinakis, Gene Mappin, Steve Jordan, Ken Comer, Mike Lambert, Rick Coyle, Dan Pinkerton, Larry Hayes, Paul Heron, Mary Jo Cervantes, Tom Turnbull, Joe Aldridge, and so many more. It was an honor and a privilege to serve with them.

A renowned leadership consultant in her own right, Michele Jackman, was a great friend and mentor. I continue to rely on her wisdom and sage advice.

Last, but certainly not least, my wife, Yolanda, has been my rock, providing me with love and support. And I was blessed with four great children, now in their 30s: Molly, Kelly, Patrick, and John. They made me want to become a better man so that I could be a better father. I never fully reached that goal, but I'm still trying.

Introduction

*D*ust *Thou Art: Finding God, Happiness, and Fulfillment* is my third book. I had just completed the manuscript for it and *Leave a Legacy: Reflections on the Strategies of Great Leadership* in February of 2003 when my good friend and classmate from the Naval Academy, Captain Perry Martini, called me on the phone and said, "Stew, we should write a book together."

I told him I had just completed rough drafts of two books, but I would be happy to put them on the back burner in order to collaborate with him on what became *Inspiring Leadership: Character and Ethics Matter*, published in November of 2004.

Now, after all these years, I felt it was time to go back to work on *Dust Thou Art*. (*Leave a Legacy* was published earlier this year.) Even though it had been in hibernation, so to speak, it still influenced many of my thoughts in *Inspiring Leadership*.

From my earliest days, I have always been a student of leadership. I guess it started in grade school when I was elected president of my fourth grade class. Anyone who attended parochial schools in the 1950s can probably relate to those formative years.

One of the duties of the class president was to come to the front of the room and keep order whenever "the good sister," a Catholic nun, left the room. The president was required to write the names of "kids who talked" on the blackboard, a thankless task and certainly not one to enhance your popularity.

Needless to say, when it came time to elect a new president for the second semester, Stew Fisher lost, in a landslide, to Ken Ray, an ignominious end to my early aspirations for political office. That was my first leadership lesson, and there were many more to come. (Humorous footnote: Ken Ray's popularity sank like mine as he dutifully wrote the names of various miscreants on the blackboard in the teacher's absence during that second semester. I guess he didn't learn from my mistake either.)

There have been many more leadership lessons during my time on the planet: camp counselor, senior class president, indoctrinating new plebes (freshmen) at the Naval Academy, Commanding Officer of a combat search and rescue squadron during Desert Storm, to name a few. Each experience had something to teach me.

I also tried to study the great leaders in history to find out what made them so influential and inspiring: Hannibal, Alexander the Great, George Washington, Abraham Lincoln, Robert E. Lee, Teddy Roosevelt, Gandhi, John F. Kennedy, Mother Teresa, Martin Luther King, Ronald Reagan, Coach John Wooden, and Pope John Paul II. Of course, the greatest of them all was Jesus Christ.

Over time, through my own real life experiences,

observing inspirational leaders in action, and the study of great leaders before me, I developed my own leadership philosophy. Probably the best teacher has been my own leadership mistakes.

There's no reason for any aspiring leader to make the same mistakes that I did. That is one of the principle reasons for writing this book, and I hope it will be of help to you as we explore the art of leadership together.

But on a deeper level, I also wanted to explore the soul-searching questions man has asked himself since he first walked upright and, most importantly, examine his relationship to a loving God. I hope it will be and insightful look at what it means to be human and why we are here.

I feel there is a wonderful purpose for our existence, but it cannot be fulfilled without a strong connection to Almighty God. Disconnected from Him, "we are nothing more than dust." But in concert with Him, we can achieve the greatness He intended for each of us.

To be sure, we often stumble. We can be weak, proud, arrogant, cruel, lazy, and unfeeling. But we can also be generous, strong, selfless, creative, kind, and loving. We only rise to our best selves when we seek God's help. Apart from Him, we are nothing.

Great leaders spend their entire lifetimes working on self-improvement. They certainly can't lead others until they have mastered themselves. They lead by example and adhere to the highest standards of conduct.

But without the help of a loving God, this lifelong quest for self-improvement and inspiring leadership is destined to fail. If we begin to think that we can do it on our own, we're sadly mistaken, and we will quickly lose our way. It's important to remember that God seldom shouts at us, but rather talks in a whisper to the depths of our souls. The ability to listen to that whisper makes all the difference in the world!

Jesus, God's Gift to Mankind

The birth of Jesus is, without a doubt, the central event in all of human history! Think of it: Nothing else has ever had such impact. It is so significant that all historical events are based on the date of His arrival, measured as either B.C. or A.D.

It is impossible for the human mind to even comprehend the enormity of it: *An Almighty God decided to bond with all of mankind!* For Him to merge His infinite power with lowly, flawed human beings—*to become one of us*—is utterly mind boggling!

Allow me to use an analogy. Imagine if you will, a man freely choosing to live all of his days as one of thousands of ants toiling in the sunless, earthen labyrinth of their colony, *for the sole purpose of showing them a better way of living.* But even that analogy fails to capture what God did for us, because the gap between God and man is *infinite* compared to that between man and the insect world. Only a God of limitless love could conceive of such a remarkable idea: sending His own Son to become one with us in every way but sin!

Why did He do this? Simply, God knew we were in deep trouble. We lived harsh, cruel, and brutal lives and were totally unaware of His existence, much less of His extraordinary plan for us. We had absolutely no concept of someone who could have this much love for us, a love so great that it *had* to be shared. To be one with Him would result in unimaginable happiness for us, but we had no way of knowing that until He revealed it through His own Son.

What is even more remarkable about God's plan was that He knew, long ahead of time, that His Son, Jesus, would have to endure unspeakable torture and an ignominious death on a cross at the hands of His enemies in order for the plan to be fulfilled. And yet, both Father and Son were committed, without reservation, to this extraordinary way to save mankind. Just think for a moment of the magnitude of this undertaking. For those of us who are fathers, I doubt if we could ever allow one of our own sons to be sacrificed in this horrific way—or even conceive of such a plan! The idea is utterly beyond our comprehension. Even more astonishing, God could have used *any other method* to save us, but His love was so great that *He purposely chose this one!*

God first revealed this remarkable plan to Abraham, the patriarch of the Jewish nation. He told him that He would bring His own Son into the world through Abraham's descendants.

Many generations later, just as God had promised, Jesus Christ came to earth a tiny babe on that first Christmas. He could have arrived in kingly splendor, befitting the God-man He was, but instead chose the humblest of ways. Without a place to call His own, He was born in a stable, borrowed for the night.

And from the very beginning, this "Light of the World" came under attack by the forces of evil, intent on snuffing Him out before His message of love, the "good news," could be delivered. King Herod, told of this potential rival by the Wise Men from the East, sought to murder Him in His crib. Fortunately, Joseph, the foster father of Jesus, was warned of Herod's monstrous plan in a dream and escaped with the mother and child into Egypt. Only after Herod's death, could the family safely return to a normal life in their hometown of Nazareth. There, Joseph taught his young Son the skills of a carpenter.

The only account we have of Jesus as a youth is the family pilgrimage to Jerusalem when He was twelve years old. When the Passover feast was over, Mary and Joseph began the trek home to Nazareth in a caravan of family and friends, the customary way to travel in those days. Thinking that their Son was probably with other relatives in the group, He wasn't missed at first. But to their horror, they soon discovered Jesus was not with them. They began a frantic search for Him from one end of the caravan to the other. Deeply distraught now, they could only conclude that He had stayed behind. They must hurry back to Jerusalem, for who knew what could happen to a young boy of twelve in that huge city? Would they even be able to find Him? As parents, their hearts sank.

After three days of searching the crowded streets, they finally came upon their young Son in the temple, questioning and teaching the elders.

These learned men were astounded at Jesus' wisdom as they sat mesmerized by His brilliance. These were the wisest men in all of Israel, and yet, Jesus' knowledge eclipsed their own. Where could a mere boy of twelve acquire such insight they wondered, knowledge they had not yet discovered in a whole lifetime of study!

Mary approached her Son, anguish clearly written on her face, "Son, why have You done this to us? Your father and I have been looking for You with great anxiety." He replied, "Why were you looking for Me? Did you not know that I must be in My Father's house?" The underlying message was clear. Already He had begun His earthly mission: bringing the good news to a world desperately needing hope and a better way of life.

Jesus' response was not intended as an insult to His parents or an affront to their authority. He was simply revealing what He had come on earth to do. For next we read that "He went down with them and came to Nazareth, and was obedient to them; and His mother kept all of these things in her heart. And Jesus advanced in wisdom and age and favor before God and man." Throughout His life, Jesus taught mainly by example. Here He was, God incarnate, yet obedient to His human parents. What a lesson in humility and obedience!

We don't hear another word about the Savior of Mankind until He began His public ministry at the age of thirty. For all those intervening years, He had labored in anonymity as a carpenter, working alongside His father, Joseph, in their small shop in Nazareth. No doubt, He was a strong and able craftsman serving His friends and relatives there. But no one ever realized that the long-awaited Messiah was in their midst. And the Son of God never chose to reveal His almighty divinity in all those years among them.

For centuries, the Jewish people had waited for God's promise to Abraham to be fulfilled. Because they expected an earthly king, robed in splendor, to deliver them from the occupying Romans, they failed to recognize the meek and humble man who came instead. Jesus was simply not the one they were looking for. *This was certainly no king!*

Jesus began His public ministry at the Jordan River where He sought out His cousin, John, who was there baptizing repentant sinners to prepare them for the imminent arrival of the Messiah. Certainly not needing to atone for any sins Himself, He nevertheless allowed John to baptize Him as a demonstration of the need for all people to seek reconciliation with God and forgiveness for their sins. Time and again, Jesus would use *example* as His most powerful teaching tool.

Jesus was unlike any teacher they had ever seen. He taught radical ideas of "loving your enemies" and "turning the other cheek." He carried no money and His earthly possessions were the clothes on His back. He befriended the outcasts of society: sinners, beggars, prostitutes, lepers, tax collectors, the sick, the infirm, the dying, and even those possessed by the devil. He performed astonishing miracles for people suffering lifelong afflictions: curing the lame and the blind, healing the sick, casting out demons, and even bringing the dead back to life.

As Jesus' reputation grew, huge crowds would follow Him just to hear His message of hope. They were uplifted by His telling of an Almighty Father who loved them so much He had prepared a place for them for all eternity, so magnificent that "eye had not seen, nor ear heard" anything like it before. It was a place of joy and happiness beyond their wildest imaginings, and they would share it with a wonderful God *forever*. Jesus reassured them that the pains and sufferings of daily life were only temporary and that a much better existence awaited all those willing to follow Him.

Jesus never said that His way would be easy. But He did promise that they would always have the help they needed. God's love would get them through any trials they might face. They only had to ask and then have the confidence that He would take care of them.

If people had any doubt who their Heavenly Father was or what He was like, Jesus simply told them, "He who sees Me, also sees the Father." They no longer had to wonder about the nature of this loving God. Simply by watching Jesus, they would know He was kind, patient, loving, selfless, and compassionate. He was totally different from the false gods worshiped at the time: Baal, Jupiter, Neptune, Zeus, Athena, Pan, and other bronze and marble images. This was a real and living God who cared about each of them as a father would his own children, who found joy in their joy, success in their success, and tears in their sorrow.

Jesus always spoke the truth and often angered the privileged elite, telling them what hypocrites they were. Deep down, they knew He was right about them, and their resentment grew into hatred. *How dare He expose them!* They had to get rid of this troublemaker once and for all; they had to kill Him.

Assembling enough liars to falsely testify against Jesus, they convinced the Romans to condemn Him and allow Him to be crucified. But first they had Jesus scourged. Scourging, at the time of the Roman occupation, was one of the cruelest of punishments. It literally tore a man apart and was a death sentence in itself. *Men did not survive scourging!*

Afterward, to add to Jesus' pain, His torturers fashioned a crown of thorns and pressed it into His skull, mocking Him, striking Him, and spitting on Him. And all the while, *the God who created the entire universe* sat humbly silent. He could have summoned legions of angels to slay His tormentors on the spot, but chose humility instead.

Jesus had to carry His own cross to His execution, totally abandoned by all of His friends and followers. Fearing He would die before they could make Him endure the horror and humiliation of crucifixion, His executioners grabbed a stranger from the crowd to help Jesus with His cross.

At the execution site, Golgotha, they stripped Him of His garments, tearing away scabs and raw flesh, and cruelly threw Him down on His cross. Men then drove nails, *the size of railroad spikes*, through His hands and feet. Hoisted upright, Jesus felt the unimaginable pain of those nails through His body. Crucifixion was one of the most ignominious, horrific, and excruciating forms of execution ever devised by man. And *Jesus Himself chose that way to die.*

Jesus came into the world with nothing; He died with nothing. But during His thirty-three years on earth, He taught us, through His example, who our Father is and how much He loves us. "He who sees Me, sees the Father." He triumphed over death and showed us how to live our lives so that we may one day spend eternity with Him in heaven. *And He promised never to abandon us.*

In this incredible bond with all mankind, Jesus also became our Brother. At the same time, He made His Father, our Father, and told us to call God by the affectionate name, Abba ("Dad"). While He may not answer our prayers in the way we want Him to, *He will always answer them—in His way and in His time.*

Jesus knows each of us better than we know ourselves; He knows what we need, before we even ask. Yet, He is always eager to hear from us, "24/7."

We need only have a conversation with Him, *and He doesn't care what words we use*.

We must never forget Jesus' message for those who follow Him, "Eye has not seen, nor ear heard, the place My Father has prepared for you." *With a God like that, who endured unimaginable suffering just to bring us this encouraging message, how can we ever fear anything!*

Mary, the Mother of God

The amazing plan that God had for all of mankind would have been impossible without the cooperation of a human mother, Mary. One can imagine the astonishment of this young Jewish girl on the night she was visited by God's messenger, the Archangel Gabriel, and told that God wanted *her* to be the mother of His Son. "You will conceive a Son and you will name Him Jesus," he told her.

Of course, Mary knew Jewish tradition and was well aware of the promise of a Messiah made to Abraham so many generations ago, but she could hardly believe that she herself would be the living instrument of its fulfillment. Furthermore, how could she bear a son when she "did not know man." Although betrothed to Joseph, they had not yet lived together as husband and wife.

Gabriel comforted her, "Fear not, Mary, for you have found great favor with God. Blessed are you among women, and blessed is the fruit of your womb, Jesus."

Now the pivotal moment in all of human history had arrived. God was not about to *force* Mary's collaboration in the great miracle of the ages. She, like all other human beings, had been given His gift of free will. It would be *her choice alone* to accept the role as mother of the Savior of Mankind. She would never be coerced, for that is not the way of a loving God.

Mary's simple reply, "I am the handmaid of the Lord; be it done unto me according to His will," opened the door to a new era in human history. Mankind would never be the same. At that instant in time, in the small village of Nazareth, the Son of God merged His divinity with man, now a tiny embryo in His mother's womb. Without Mary's consent, none of this would have been possible.

So Mary now carried the Light of the World within her womb and later gave birth to Him on that cold Christmas night in Bethlehem. She shared the awesome responsibility all mothers feel toward their children as their protectors and nurturers, but even more so, knowing that her child was the hope of mankind. At Jesus' dedication in the temple, a few short days after His birth, Mary must have been frightened to hear Simeon, a holy man of God, tell her that a "sword would pierce her heart." This prediction meant that she would witness much cruelty inflicted upon her Son in the years ahead. His pain would be her pain; His suffering, her suffering.

Simeon's words came true all too quickly as she and Joseph had to flee with her newborn Son to Egypt to escape the murderous wrath of King Herod. And later, imagine the worry and grief she felt when she lost her twelve-year-old boy in the huge Passover crowds of Jerusalem. She was His mother and guardian. But now she had no idea where the

Son she loved—and the Savior of Mankind!—was. She and Joseph searched frantically for three days before finding Him. Once more, that sword had to pierce her heart.

Back in Nazareth, Mary watched Jesus grow into manhood. No doubt, like all mothers, she comforted Him when He cried, kissed His bruises to make them better, tickled Him, rocked Him in her arms, cooked His meals, and taught Him how to help with the chores. They must have talked and laughed together often as the bond between them grew. Even before His ministry was supposed to begin, Jesus responded to His mother's plea and performed His first miracle *for her*, changing water into wine at the wedding feast in Cana. Their mutual affection and devotion was very strong, especially now that her husband, Joseph, had died and they only had each other.

During Jesus' three-year public ministry, His mother was always close by. At the end, when His betrayer, Judas, turned Him over to His enemies, Mary never left His side. She witnessed her Son's cruel scourging and heard the people whom He had once healed scream, "Crucify him!" She followed His torturous steps to Calvary, and while other followers scattered like frightened sheep, she stood courageously at the foot of the cross. Before drawing His last, painful breath, Mary heard Jesus say to His disciple, John, "Son, behold thy mother," and to her, "Mother, behold thy son." At that moment, Jesus shared His last greatest gift with us: He made His mother the mother of all mankind.

As He was taken down from the cross, she held her Son's bruised and battered body in her arms one last time. Once again, as Simeon had predicted, a final sword pierced her grief-stricken heart.

But when Jesus arose from the dead three days later, His triumph became her triumph. Just as He promised never to abandon us, so too is His mother—now *our* mother—there to help. She has appeared numerous times to encourage us and renew our faith: Mexico City, Lourdes, and Fatima to name just three. She truly listens to our prayers. And befitting the Mother of Jesus, she is the only human being never tainted by sin. She provides us with an eternal connection to her Son. We owe her a great debt of gratitude, for without Mary, the salvation miracle would never have happened. She is the Mother of God, and just as remarkably, *our* mother, too.

Joseph, Foster Father of Jesus

Very little is known about Joseph, the foster father of Jesus. The Bible simply says, "He was a just man." We can, however, surmise a few things about him.

When Joseph discovered that his betrothed, Mary, was already pregnant, he could have followed Jewish law and had her stoned immediately for her infidelity. Instead, he decided to keep her secret and raise the child as his own, with no one in their small town of Nazareth the wiser.

Later, when the Angel of the Lord appeared to him in a dream and told him the true identity of the child, he fully accepted his role as foster father and guardian of the Son of God. This was certainly was no small undertaking! That God personally chose him for this role tells us that Joseph had very special qualities. It also reveals the depth of Joseph's faith and his dedication to Mary and the infant Jesus.

Later, when King Herod threatened the life of his family, it took great courage for Joseph to pack up all their belongings, in the dead of night, and leave familiar surroundings for the uncertain life of immigrants in a foreign land, Egypt. Indeed, crossing the Sinai Desert—on foot with a woman and a small child!—was no small feat, even by today's standards.

Back in Nazareth, after the danger to Jesus had

passed with the death of King Herod, we can imagine Joseph's strong and skilled hands guiding those of his foster Son as they sanded and shaped the wood of a sturdy table for one of the neighbors. I'm sure they became a well-known and greatly appreciated team in their Nazareth carpenter shop as Jesus grew into manhood. No doubt, working side by side all those years, a strong bond of affection and mutual admiration developed between them.

When Joseph died years later, it had to be a sad time for Mary and Jesus, for they were a close family. The foster father of the Son of God had to be a man of faith, courage, warmth, dedication, skill and physical strength, just based on what little we know of him. Would God the Father have entrusted His Son to anyone less!

Letting Go and Letting God

All of us like to be free and in control of our own destiny. No one can do it better than we can. Or so we think.

But God has a master plan for each one of us. We just don't realize it yet. Truth is, God knows us better than we know ourselves. He knows what we need better than we know what to ask for. In fact, not a thing we do goes unnoticed by God. He watches over our every action. As Jesus tells us, "He even counts the hairs on our heads." And as much as He cares for all the animals of His creation, He cares for us even more. Our human minds will never be able to fathom the extent of His love for us. It is beyond our comprehension. It is infinite and boundless.

Perhaps our lack of understanding and inability to appreciate the depth of His love for us explains why it is so difficult to put ourselves entirely in His care and to trust in His plan. But if we fully realized Who God is, we would easily let go and let Him take charge of our lives. Instead, we cling to that all-precious control, feeling that we can do a better job than He can, unwilling to submit our will to His.

Every once in a while, however, we reach a low point in our lives that proves to be a blessing in disguise. We discover our own helplessness, our total inability to go it alone. Overcome by events and not knowing where to turn, we cry out for help. It is then that we discover what a Champion we have in God. When all seems lost, He pulls us out of our despair and takes us where we need to go. His guidance, His healing, His renewal makes us wonder why we didn't ask for His help in the first place. By experiencing troubled times, we learn to rely on His almighty power, for *nothing* is impossible to God. His artistry knows no bounds.

Sometimes God's solution is baffling to us and totally unexpected. The answer to our prayers ends up being something we would never have dreamed of. We are lifted to a new place that we never even thought to go. Yet it is far better than the destination we were seeking had we been left to our own devices. The old saying, "Be careful what you pray for; it might be granted to you," takes on a new meaning. *After the fact*, we discover that what we *thought* we needed would have been totally wrong for us.

This teaches us a new way to pray to God. Rather than reciting a litany of the things we *think* we need from Him to make us happy, we simply rely on the familiar prayer Jesus taught us, "Not my will, but *Your* will be done." It's as simple as that. Say that short prayer with the absolute confidence that God knows what's best for us, and then get out of His way and let Him go to work. Granted, this is a leap of faith that most of us are uncomfortable with at first. But it's amazing what happens when we give it a try. "The Lord works in mysterious ways, His wonders to perform." He will astound us with the solutions

He provides for us. It is the only real "magic" that exists.

Keep in mind that God usually reaches us with a whisper rather than a shout. Often it is a thought or an idea that He plants quietly in our minds. We might call it intuition. Or perhaps He sends another person into our lives to interact with us for His specific purpose. For example, out of the blue, we may get a phone call from someone we haven't heard from in a long time. Or maybe a perfect stranger comes into our lives and has a dramatic effect on us. At the time, we don't even recognize that this is God at work. It is only upon later reflection that we see what really happened and Who was the catalyst.

Sometimes God "gets the ball rolling" by giving us a *restless spirit*. We can't quite put our finger on it, but we get an uneasy feeling that our lives need to change. We begin to listen to our inner souls and ask questions. This restless search for answers is just what God intended, for it opens us up to His whisper and allows His Spirit to move us.

It would be nice to claim that we always "let go and let God." The truth is, that doesn't happen very often. We're "serial meddlers." We're always "mucking it up," trying to do things *our way*. However, when we *do* let God have a free hand in our lives and get out of His way, things change for the better, *every single time*.

Even the Saints Were Sinners

With only one exception, Mary, the Mother of God, no human being who ever walked the face of the earth was without sin. That's a very poor batting average for Homo sapiens! Indeed, we are flawed and imperfect creatures. But perhaps there is some good news in that sad statistic: We must rely on a loving God to perfect us and make us whole, to heal our brokenness.

It's interesting to note that some of the greatest saints in history certainly didn't start out that way. Saint Paul began as Saul, a Roman citizen whose sole purpose in life was to root out Christians and put them to death. In his case, God intervened in a most dramatic way, knocking him from his horse and blinding him. "Saul, Saul, why do you persecute me?" the Lord's asked. "Who are you, Lord?" was Saul's reply. God then instructed him to go into Damascus and seek out a holy Christian man named Ananias who would instruct him in his new found faith. Imagine Ananias's shock when confronted by Saul, this dangerous persecutor of Christians. He had to be highly skeptical of Saul's real motives. Was this just a ruse to deceive and capture more of his Christian brethren?

But Saul's change of faith was genuine, and he became Saint Paul, spending the rest of his life teaching the Gospel of Jesus Christ throughout

Greece, Rome, and Asia Minor. He was shipwrecked, scourged, beaten, imprisoned, and finally beheaded. But as he himself would say, "I have fought the good fight; I have run the good race; and I will receive the crown of glory."

Saint Augustine was far from being a saint in his youth. He was a carouser, a drunken reveler, and fathered an illegitimate child. No one would have mistaken him for a saint in those early days. But his mother, Saint Monica, never gave up on him and prayed her entire life that God would transform her son and pull him up from his debauchery. God heard her prayers and Augustine became one of the church's greatest philosophers and theologians, a "Doctor of the Church."

Next we have the good thief on the cross, one of two criminals crucified on either side of Jesus. While the other, unrepentant thief berated the Lord, cynically urging Jesus to save all three of them, "If You're the Son of God, why don't You save us?" The good thief told him to be silent, "Have you no fear of God? This Man is innocent, but we deserve our fate." Then turning to Jesus he said, "Lord, remember me when You come into Your kingdom." And Jesus replied, "I assure you, this day you will be with Me in Paradise." It simply proves that God's ability to save us knows no bounds. Even after a lifetime of crime, He can make us saints, if we're willing to believe in Him.

These are just three examples, but there are many

more. No saint was without his faults. Some could once be described as evil. But somehow each of them managed to connect with God in a unique way and allow Him to use them for His purposes. They became instruments in the Lord's hands. In many cases, their transformations were astonishing and miraculous.

If God can work such wonders, why not let Him do the same in our own lives? We need only have faith—and then get out of His way!

God's Justice, Mercy, and Grace

Free will is one of God's special gifts to mankind. He could easily have created human beings that would *robotically* follow a righteous path and do His will unfailingly and without question. Like His other creatures, He could have made us so that we reacted solely on instinct. However, God wanted more than that for us. He wanted people to respond to Him *through their own choice,* not because they *had* to. This ability to choose, or free will, means that bad choices can also be made. Man can just as easily choose evil instead of good, and sadly, he often does.

When human beings get themselves into trouble, the first question that is often asked is, "Why did God let this happen?" The truth is, if He didn't, He would rob us of our free will, the key attribute that makes us human. God wants us to do good works and return His love, but only if it's *voluntary.* But the very fact that we can choose evil means that there must be consequences for wrong behavior. God is certainly no pushover. He is also a just God. If we freely choose to go against His will, we will experience that justice.

Fortunately for us, God is also kind and merciful. When mankind stumbles, He often lets us off the hook, handling us much more gently than we deserve. He has done this throughout history, from the Israelites of the Old Testament to the present day.

Many of our insights into who God is and what He is like, especially attributes such as His kindness and mercy, come to us from observing His Son, Jesus Christ. After all, it was Jesus who told us, "He who sees Me also sees the Father." As He drew His last breath, in excruciating pain nailed to a rough wooden cross, He called out, "Father, forgive them, for they know not what they do." It's frightening to contemplate what our punishment *should have been* for torturing and crucifying the Son of God.

Another imponderable aspect of our amazing God is the grace He bestows on each one of us. Think of grace as a free gift with no strings attached. By definition, it's nothing we *earned*, and certainly nothing we *deserve*. It can come in many forms: peace of mind, help in times of trouble, good health, His mercy, an insight to a problem, or freedom from want, to name just a few. And let us not forget the greatest of all, the gift of His Son, Jesus. Truly, "our cup runneth over" with the graces we have received from our loving God.

Perhaps we can look at grace and mercy in another way. It is sometimes said that mercy is God *not giving us what we deserve*, and grace is God *giving us what we don't deserve*. That's a good way to sum it up.

The Faith of Abraham and Job

Two of the most interesting figures of the Bible were Abraham and Job. We marvel at their faith in God.

Consider first Abraham. Here he was, a Bedouin of ancient Mesopotamia living in the town of Ur. Through him, God would introduce Himself to the human race. At the time, Abram, his name before his encounter with God, was leading a typical nomadic life, tending his flocks just as generations of his forefathers had done in centuries past. Imagine his astonishment when God appeared to him and identified Himself as the one, true God. Like other Bedouin sheepherders of the day, Abram probably had *many* gods that he worshiped. Now he was being told that there was only one.

God went on to say that Abram would be the leader of a great nation that God would make His chosen people, and that he would henceforth be called Abraham. Furthermore, his descendants would be as numerous as the stars in the heavens. Now this last prediction was indeed astonishing, for Abraham was very old and his wife, Sarah, was far beyond her child-bearing years. How could this be possible!

But that wasn't all. God wanted Abraham to leave his ancestral home and journey with his flocks and all his possessions to the place God had reserved for His future people, the "Promised Land," in distant

Canaan. It would be a land "flowing with milk and honey."

So what did Abraham do after this astonishing encounter with God? In a supreme act of faith, he did just what was asked of him. Lock, stock, and barrel he uprooted his family and traveled to distant Canaan. And just as God had promised, He rewarded Abraham's faithfulness with a strong baby boy, Isaac.

After living in the Promised Land for a number of years, God tested Abraham's faith one more time. He told Abraham to build an altar and use it to *sacrifice his only son as an offering to God*. Imagine what this meant to Abraham. Here God had promised him that his descendants would be as numerous as the stars, and now he was being asked to terminate that future lineage!

Abraham's heart must have been heavy as he set to work building the altar, his young son at his side helping him gather the wood for its construction. His mind must have been racing, "Why am I being asked to do such a thing?" And yet, when the work was done, he obediently laid his beloved son on the altar and raised his knife to complete the onerous task. Just before the blade descended to end Isaac's life, an angel of the Lord stayed Abraham's hand. This was only meant to be a test of Abraham's faith. Isaac's life was spared and God's promise to Abraham would be fulfilled.

We have to marvel at Abraham's continuing faith in God. First, he accepted the Lord as the one, true

God, never having known of Him before. Then, at the Lord's bidding, he willingly moved with all his possessions, flocks, and aging wife, Sarah, to a distant and unfamiliar land. And finally, he agreed to sacrifice his only son in obedience to God's wishes.

Next, we have Job, another man of amazing faith. Job was blessed by God: seven sons, three daughters, 7,000 sheep, 3,000 camels, 700 yoke of oxen, 500 donkeys, and a large number of servants. He was blameless and upright and the greatest man among all the people of the East.

God was proud of Job and bragged of this upright man to Satan. But Satan countered that Job was a good and righteous man only because he was prosperous. Take away his prosperity, Satan predicted, and he would *curse* God.

So God allowed Satan to take away Job's wealth and possessions and then permitted a strong desert wind to collapse the house where his ten children were celebrating a feast together, killing them all. Despite these calamities, Job's faith in God was unshaken. So Satan next asked God to allow him to attack Job's health in order to further test the good man's loyalty and perseverance. God allowed it but told Satan not to kill him. Job was then covered with painful sores from the top of his head to the soles of his feet. Even though confused by the reasons for his afflictions—since he had done nothing wrong to deserve such misfortune—Job remained steadfast and loyal to God.

As a reward for his faith, even after enduring the calamities inflicted upon him by Satan, God made Job even more prosperous than before and blessed him with seven new sons and three new daughters. Job enjoyed great longevity and lived to see four generations of his offspring.

So what do these two men of the Bible have to teach us in the 21st Century? Simply, to have unshakeable trust in God and put our faith in His plan for each of us, even when that plan is beyond our understanding.

Have a Daily Conversation
with God

Most of us, from the time we were youngsters, were taught to pray. We grew up with familiar favorites such as "The Lord's Prayer" and "The Hail Mary." They even became part of our culture. For example, we use "The Hail Mary" to describe a last second desperation pass at the end of a football game.

While these "structured prayers" are certainly worthwhile, God listens to *all* prayers, and I suspect He especially likes those prayers that are simply spontaneous conversations with Him. They needn't be eloquent or poetic either, merely sincere words from the heart, however we might choose to express them.

I doubt if length matters much to God either. For example, maybe we simply cry out, "Help me!" as our car skids on a patch of ice. Or maybe we just tell Him about our day, the highs, the lows, what made us laugh, what we accomplished, what we still need to do, how we might need His help, etc. I suspect idle ramblings are just as important to God as eloquence. He just wants to hear our thoughts and accepts us warts and all. My guess is that our loving God is simply glad to connect with us in *any* way, *whenever* we choose to talk to Him, and His line is open 24/7. One thing is for certain, He never puts us on hold.

It's hard for us to grasp this simple truth: *God knows us far better than we know ourselves, and He knows what we need better than we know what to ask for*. In fact, that may be the reason our prayers sometimes go unanswered. He knows that what we might pray for is just the *opposite* of what we really need. Or maybe the timing is simply off. His reply to our entreaties is not necessarily a "no," just a "not yet."

But be assured that God *does* hear our prayers whether He chooses to act on them immediately or not. Even though we sometimes feel that God is "distant," He is always within earshot and *is* listening. Most importantly, He always has our best interests at heart. And as we said before, even though He knows what we need before we ask, He still wants to hear from us. He also rewards persistence. Sometimes it takes years of prayer to get the answer we seek, just as Saint Monica prayed much of her life for her wayward son, Saint Augustine. But eventually the answer will come, and with God's help, we will recognize it.

The Eternal Soul, Our Connection to God

Human beings are composed of body, mind, *and* spirit. This last element is our immortal soul. I believe this is our direct connection to God. God placed in each of us a *Piece of Himself.* It is an awe-inspiring concept that is difficult, if not impossible, for us to grasp. It is nothing short of a miracle that He shared His divinity with us in this way. It explains why man, throughout his existence on earth and in all cultures, has always sought a Supreme Being. He is hardwired to reconnect with his Maker.

The ultimate reconnection can only occur in heaven after our mortal lives on earth are done. At that time we will have achieved our ultimate destiny: the total happiness and fulfillment of being one with God. Perhaps this is also why Hell is the ultimate punishment, for the soul will forever be separated from the one thing that can make it whole and complete. This means eternal anguish.

Many of the soul's characteristics deal with intangibles. We know that God implanted a conscience in the soul, since even the most primitive societies have a sense of right and wrong. We know that the soul is also capable of love, friendship, and loyalty. And like its Maker, the soul is eternal; our spirits will never die.

Our most altruistic inclinations spring from the soul: kindness, mercy, forgiveness, justice, fairness, and decency. In short, all those things that reflect God in us are part of the soul. This makes sense because God made us to be like Him in everything but sin.

God implanted a wonderful homing device, the soul, in each one of us. We can follow its guidance or not. But in the end, we will exercise our free will and make one of two choices: join our souls with God and live forever in happiness, or live apart from Him in despair and anguish for all eternity.

Three Divine Persons
in One God

While the human mind can never fully comprehend and appreciate the mystery of God, it doesn't mean that we can't know *something* about Him. Just as a good tracker can read footprints left in the snow and know about the animal that passed by, God has left clues for us as well.

Without a doubt, our best source of knowledge about God is His Son, Jesus Christ, Who told us, "He who sees Me, sees the Father." That alone provides us with a wealth of information and insight. Up until then, we only had the writings of Jewish authors of the Old Testament. Their accounts go all the way back to God's creation of the world and Adam and Eve, Noah and the Great Flood, and then follow the history of the Israelites from Abraham to the Messiah.

The God of the Old Testament was awesomely powerful and sometimes intimidating, whether it was parting the Red Sea, appearing as a pillar of fire leading the Israelites in their forty-year exodus from Egypt, decimating opposing armies as the Israelites fought to take over the Promised Land, or raining down fire and brimstone on ancient Sodom and Gomorrah. Perhaps the Jews of the Old Testament needed that type of "tough love" from God because they could indeed be a stubborn and "stiff-necked" people.

In the New Testament, we see another side of God in the Person of His Son, Jesus Christ. Jesus tells us, "Learn from Me, for I am meek and humble of heart." This is a far different image than the fire and brimstone we saw in the Old Testament. Now we are shown the depth of God's compassion and love for man as Jesus mourns the death of His friend, Lazarus. In fact, the shortest sentence in the Bible tells us poignantly, "Jesus wept." In further accounts of Jesus' life on earth, we are given a wealth of new insights into the nature of God: His love for children, His concern for the downtrodden, the poor, and the infirm, His patient teaching of His disciples, His warmth and humanity, and His willingness to forgive, even those who crucified and abandoned Him.

But we also learn that Jesus was no pushover. The Son of God courageously challenged the rich, the proud, and the powerful, letting them know what hypocrites they were. And, in righteous anger, He didn't hesitate to drive the money changers from His "Father's House," the temple, whipping their backsides as He turned over the tables holding their merchandise.

But the greatest miracle embodied in the Son of God is the merging of two distinct natures: the nature of God and the nature of man. *The very same God who created the universe, humbled Himself to share in our humanity!* No event in human history will ever equal this. And apart from His divine nature, Jesus experienced all the travails of any man. He got tired, cold, and hungry, and felt despair, disappointment, and betrayal. But He overcame all the weaknesses of His human nature, and thus showed us how to do the same ourselves.

So far we have focused on God the Father and God the Son, but what of the Third Person in the Blessed Trinity, the Holy Spirit? In the mystery of the nature of God, He is the least known. But while a mystery, it doesn't mean that we know nothing about Him. We are told that He was the Voice of God speaking through the prophets of the Old Testament and that Mary conceived Jesus "by the power of the Holy Spirit." He often comes like a powerful wind or a pillar of fire. After the crucifixion and death of Jesus, His appearance in tongues of fire over the heads of the apostles gave them courage when, just before, they had been cowering in fear. It has also been said that the love of the Father for the Son and the Son for the Father is a manifestation of the Holy Spirit.

Men through the ages have struggled to explain the unexplainable, the nature of Three Persons in one God. Saint Patrick of Ireland used the three leaves of the shamrock to illustrate this mystery. Some have said it is like striking three keys on the piano to make one chord. Others have likened the Trinity to the merging of the tips of three burning candles to form one brilliant flame.

Despite all of these explanations, the mystery of God remains. Our human minds are not up to the task of defining His infinite perfection. He has given us some knowledge of Who He is, but the rest will remain hidden until we meet Him face to face in eternity. Until then, we can take immense joy in the fact that God loves us beyond anything we can possibly imagine and wants us to be united with Him in heaven forever.

We Can Never Be the Flame, Only the Mirror

Everyone is born with certain talents, unique to each of us. We didn't do anything to earn them; they were simply given to us at birth. Can anyone deny that Michelangelo and Da Vinci had special gifts? Will there ever be another Mozart or Beethoven? And what about athletic talents? A Jim Thorpe, a Michael Jordan, or a Tiger Woods comes along once in a century. In the field of leadership, we will probably never find the equal of Abraham Lincoln, Robert E. Lee, Winston Churchill, Pope John Paul II, Mother Teresa, or Martin Luther King, Jr. Take any field of human endeavor and you will find men and women who stand out as giants.

While we ourselves may never equal the accomplishments of these great men and women, we each have our own set of talents. But what is most important is that we remember that they are truly *gifts* and never belonged to us in the first place; they are merely on loan from Almighty God. And since we had nothing to do with whatever talents and skills were given to us, to boast about them would be the height of hubris. Instead, our only goal in life should be to develop these gifts through study, practice, and hard work.

The Bible tells us, "To whom much is given,

much will be expected." It's another way of saying that there is going to be a day of reckoning. If we squander our talents by not developing them and using them, we have failed to live up to the potential our Creator put within us and will be judged accordingly.

We need to be humble because any talents that we have are *God's* gifts, not something we achieved on our own. In a way, we are like the lighthouses of old that guarded rocky shores. Each had a brilliant source of light, a bright flame if you will. But that is the Creator's light, *not ours,* that illuminates. Think of it as the flame He places in each of us. We can only be mirrors, reflecting that light source to the far horizon. In other words, we can "polish the mirror," but we are never the flame.

God wants us to use His gifts for the benefit of others. It doesn't matter whether our accomplishments are highly acclaimed or totally unheralded, monumental or seemingly insignificant. What matters is that we become mirrors of His glory, spreading His light to the far horizon. Only then will we have fulfilled our destiny on earth.

Our Connection to Those Who Have Died

By our very nature, we seem to be hardwired to believe in a hereafter, convinced that our spirits won't die but will go on forever. In fact, most of the world's great religions believe in life after death, and their followers feel a strong connection with those who have died. While we can't *physically* bridge the gap that exists between us and our departed loved ones, we still feel an intangible, *spiritual* connection to them.

Some have spoken convincingly of being visited by their loved ones in dreams so real they defied explanation. In a few instances, they were able to converse with these relatives, receive advice, comfort, and answers to their most probing questions. For most of us, however, it's not that dramatic. There's just a sense that a loved one is near and *can* hear our one-way conversations.

The Catholic Church fully supports this connection and calls it the "Mystical Body of Christ." It unifies the souls in purgatory, the saints in heaven, and human beings on earth into one, collective entity. Christ teaches us that we on earth can pray for the deliverance of the souls in purgatory—as they go through a period of purification before going to heaven—or ask for intercession and help from saints who have already been united with God.

Unfathomable Reward
("Eye Has Not Seen….")

We really don't know what awaits us in the hereafter. Jesus only promised us "that eye has not seen, nor ear heard the place my Father has prepared for you."

However, knowing the infinite power of Almighty God, it must be a place of unfathomable beauty, peace, and happiness. Some have even said that if we could get a glimpse of heaven while still on earth, we would be so overwhelmed that our free will could no longer function: We couldn't help but always choose the good and seek a righteous path in our lives.

Since happiness could not be complete without our loved ones, I'm convinced that there will be a grand reunion with them in heaven. In fact, those who have had near death experiences tell us that beloved relatives were the first people they met after they were pronounced "clinically dead." They also describe being drawn to a Being of intense light and experiencing a sense of total peace and loving acceptance.

After being revived and reentering their human bodies, they all felt a strong sense of longing for the heaven they had only briefly experienced. Most said that they would have preferred not to have been resuscitated, to "stay in the light," but they were told that their work on earth was not yet complete. All of them said their lives were changed forever. They no longer feared death and rededicated themselves to righteous lives that would merit a return to heaven.

Be a Better Person Today Than You Were Yesterday

Progress and improvement often seem like elusive goals. We try, we fail, we rise, we fall, and don't seem to get much better. But success is usually the last event in a long string of failures. Every setback has its own set of lessons for us if we pay attention. In fact, learning to handle failure is an important life lesson in itself. We learn to become resilient and accept disappointment as part of the human condition. We discover a very important fact: *We're not perfect, and never will be!* We also learn another vital lesson: *We need others and they need us.* We can never reach our full potential *alone*. Life is not a solo effort.

We also begin to rely on a force outside ourselves. That Force is a loving God who comes to our aid when all hope seems lost. It usually happens after our hubris has convinced us that we are self-sufficient. Our arrogance now shaken, we come to realize that we are *nothing without God.* God watches every one of our errant steps and is ready to provide the help we need if we put our faith and trust in Him. He's not expecting miracles, for He already knows us better than we know ourselves. After all, God knows what humans are all about, for He created us.

All that God asks is that we rely solely on *Him.*

He knows that we will make mistakes, but if we hang in there and keep trying, He will bring us closer to Him. After all, that's our ultimate destiny, to be one with God.

So worry less and trust God more. With His help, we only need try to be a little better today than we were yesterday. He will do the rest.

Taking Blessings for Granted

Human beings are an interesting lot. Take for example a couple on their first cruise ship vacation. They check aboard their luxury liner and are overwhelmed by the ambience and the meticulous service. They open the door to their stateroom and are amazed to see the bed turned down and a chocolate mint sitting on the pillow.

However, after a few days of this ultimate pampering and luxury, they begin to complain that the chocolate on their pillow is now too small, or that the filet mignon is "rare" when they asked for "medium rare." Even the delicious lobster tail now seems inadequate. In short, they have become jaded. What was once beyond their wildest dreams is now ordinary and doesn't measure up.

This, unfortunately, is a common experience for us all. For example, how many even consider the luxury we enjoy as a hot shower beats down on our backs? Are we even aware that the vast majority of people in the world bathe in a local river? As we browse the wide aisles of our local supermarkets with an endless variety of choices to be dropped in our shopping baskets—51 kinds of mustard, for example!—satisfying our every whim, do we even think of the many millions who haven't eaten a decent meal in a year—or even their entire lives!

If you stop and think about it, every single thing we experience in our daily lives that seems so commonplace and has escaped our notice—and appreciation!—would be considered an absolute luxury to most people in the world.

So what's the answer? I think we should begin by taking stock of the many blessings we enjoy, put them in perspective, and give thanks. When the car won't start or we get a flat tire, think of the large percentage of people in the world who don't even own an automobile. Some have never ridden in one! When you turn up the thermostat and bemoan the monthly heating bill, think of those who can't even find firewood.

After we begin to appreciate the enormous disparity that exists, it's time to loosen up the old purse strings and give more generously. And even this comes from our surplus, not from our want, and is only a small sacrifice. We have been blessed with much wealth, way out of proportion to the rest of the world. It is only right that we share this wealth and help to alleviate the poverty and suffering that exists for the majority of our fellow human beings.

Accumulating Wealth and Possessions

Accumulating wealth and possessions sometimes becomes a way of keeping score. It's a way of shouting, "Look how much money I have. I'm important. I'm *somebody!*" But there's no escaping one cold, hard fact of our time on earth: *We came into the world with nothing; we will leave with nothing.*

After all, how many homes can we live in? How many cars can we drive? How many "toys" can we use at one time? Rather than enjoying the pleasure of a nice car that handles well and fulfills their needs, some need to show off an entire *stable* of automobiles. And they are not collectors who enjoy vintage cars. They do it simply for status and "one-upsmanship."

Ever notice how the goal becomes building a yacht just a little bit longer and more expensive than someone else's? Or having a sound system costing tens of thousands of dollars, just to say they have it, when the human ear can't tell the difference anyway? Some people just can't stand the fact that their show of wealth has been eclipsed by a rival. They really don't *need* the bigger car, the bigger boat, or the bigger house. They just want to remain top dog. They seem to believe that "he who dies with the most toys wins."

But time and again it's been shown that some of the wealthiest people in the world are often the most miserable, lonely, and unfulfilled. And it's no wonder. They are totally frustrated by the fact that all their wealth can't buy one iota of happiness. They become trapped in an endless quest to accumulate more "stuff" than the next guy. And that's all it is: *stuff!*

What a terrible waste this is when there is so much poverty in the world. Once our basic needs are fulfilled, do we really need all that excess? Couldn't it be put to better use? Should there be such a disparity between the wealthy and the poor and disenfranchised of the world? Don't they also deserve to have their basic needs met: food, clothing, medical care, and a roof over their heads? Remember what Jesus told us, "What you do for the least of My brethren, you do for Me." Isn't it time we took His words to heart? Fortunately, many have. That's why philanthropists such as Bill Gates and Warren Buffet are having such impact in the world. They set an example for the rest of us. While we may not be able to donate or help as much as they do, there is always *something* we can contribute. And, if we're honest with ourselves, it's probably more than we're doing now.

In the end, we "are our brother's keeper." We will be judged not by the size of our bank accounts, but by our generosity and the size of our hearts. After all, whoever said, "You can't take it with you," was absolutely right.

Comparing Ourselves to Others

Two things can happen when we compare ourselves to others, both of them bad. Either we become arrogant, thinking we're better than everyone else, or we become jealous, worried that we're not. Comparing ourselves to others is just a huge waste of time. Working on ourselves will take an entire lifetime anyway. Trying to fix others is merely a distraction from that task.

True empowerment begins with one very powerful idea: There is no one like you in the entire universe. You are a unique creation, and the One who created you always does fantastic work. Every human being is a masterpiece. It is impossible for Him to do anything less.

The trouble starts when we forget this fundamental truth about all human beings and ourselves. Instead, we become highly critical, denying the extraordinary creations we are. It's a total waste of time and energy because it overlooks each person's uniqueness. In other words, there really is no basis for comparison. You're not better than others, you're not worse, you are simply *you*. No one like you has ever existed, and no one ever will.

Perfectionism

If a random audience were asked the question, "How many tend to be perfectionists?" there would probably be a large show of hands. To some degree or another, we all share this problem. Why? It's often because our egos won't let us admit we are anything less than perfect. It is human nature not to want to admit mistakes or shortcomings.

But perfectionism is paralyzing. To avert a mistake, we avoid making any attempt at all. For who wants to fail, look foolish, or be embarrassed? As a result, we miss out on learning new things or having breakthroughs in our lives that could change us forever. "Nothing ventured, nothing gained" is a wise saying. And yet, we try new things with great reluctance.

Perhaps the solution is to learn the value of making mistakes. Not only will it keep us humble, but it will release our creativity. All of us spend far too much time and energy worrying about mistakes and looking bad. But in truth, none of mankind's greatest achievements was ever realized without a lot of mistakes being made along the way.

Think about it: The whole history of aviation is filled with failures. Some of our earliest rockets crashed and burned on the launch pad. Many test pilots and astronauts were killed as we pushed back the frontiers of space.

Even our own experience of learning to ride a two-wheeled bike was accomplished only after numerous falls. If you did it the hard way, without training wheels, you probably scraped most of the paint off your new bike before you mastered this skill. Would you have ever guessed that learning was going on as you fell time and time again? But it was! Your subconscious mind was making adjustments after every uncoordinated spill. A wise man once said, "Take note of where you stumble; that's where the treasure lies."

Our greatest accomplishments often occur after initial failures. Thomas Edison tried ten thousand different materials for the filament of the electric light, all of them abject failures. When he was asked, "Mr. Edison, you're no better off than when you started. What have you learned?" he replied, "Well, now I know ten thousand things that don't work." That's the right attitude about making mistakes! An insightful man said, "I try to make as many mistakes as fast as I can, because that way I'll learn more quickly."

Practice was never meant to be perfect. It was meant to be a time for making mistakes and learning. After all, what is a flight instructor but a safety pilot who is there to let his student make mistakes in a safe environment?

The pursuit of perfection is *neurotic*; the pursuit of excellence, however, is a *worthy goal*. The only tragedy in making a mistake is not learning something from it. Mistakes are inevitable and, more important, vital to growth and learning. We would all have a lot less anxiety in our lives if we kept this in mind.

Aging Gracefully

I'm not sure I will ever master the art of aging gracefully. Perhaps you feel the same way. After all, what's good about getting your first pair of reading glasses, feeling those aches and pains in the morning, doing endless sit ups but still having that paunch you can't seem to get rid of, or having a person's name on the tip of your tongue but not being able to recall it? I could go on, but rather than drive us all further into depression, I'll stop there. (If, however, *you* would like to add to the list, don't let me stand in the way of your masochistic pleasure.)

As I said, I'm certainly not an expert on aging gracefully. But I think we could all agree that getting older is probably better than the alternative. So what follows are some of my thoughts and strategies that might make the journey a little easier for all of us. But be warned, this is new philosophical territory for me, so I'm winging it as I go.

First of all, if life on earth were our only reason for being, then logically, its approaching end should depress us. But God has another destiny in store for all of mankind. It is a place beyond our wildest dreams. The human mind cannot even begin to fathom what heaven must be like—and it will last *forever*!

In the grand scheme of things, our time on earth

isn't even the blink of an eye compared to all eternity. In fact, when you consider that our own solar system is a "mere" 4.5 billion years old, the human life span is even more insignificant.

Consider that the Himalayas are a *young* mountain range and still growing at the rate of a quarter inch a year. At over 29,000 feet, think how long they've been pushing their peaks toward the heavens. And as I said, they are *mere infants* compared to other mountain ranges of the world. If we can't even grasp the immensity of geological time, measured in *billions* of years, how can we possibly grasp eternity!

Think of a single ant whose sole task is to pick up *one* grain of sand from a beach on the west coast of the United States, carry it all the way across the country, and drop it on an east coast beach. He then repeats this task, one grain of sand at a time, until all the sand is transferred from the west coast to the east coast. The time that would take does not even scratch the surface of eternity. Even if you asked him to transfer *all of the sand of all of the world's beaches*, you'd still be no closer to measuring the concept of "forever."

It's all a matter of perspective. If life on earth is so short compared to *infinite joy with God for all eternity*, what good does it do to focus on something so insignificant? Now granted, we usually fail to keep this idea foremost in our minds, but if we can reflect on it more often, growing old is much less troubling.

The humorous saying, "Too soon old, too late smart," rings true for a lot of us. But hopefully, in our time on the planet, we *have* gained a bit of wisdom. We've learned not to "sweat the small stuff" and to keep things in perspective. And during those years, with any luck, we've discovered another secret to aging gracefully: *Learning should never stop.*

And as we get older, we now have more freedom to pursue knowledge that satisfies our *curiosity* rather than a curriculum of mind-numbing courses we endured to get our degrees. Learning new and challenging things sharpens the mind and keeps us young. It also adds to our store of wisdom. The human mind has an uncanny and remarkable ability to take this knowledge and weave it into interesting connections and novel ideas. While we used to think that the brain stopped making new neural pathways as we got older, science now tells us that's not true. *Our brains stop growing and age only if we let them age!*

Another bit of good news is that our bodies still respond to vigorous exercise and can remain amazingly fit even as we get older. Eighty-year-old men and women who were put on weight training programs late in life, even if they had never lifted weights before, made remarkable gains in strength and flexibility. It appears that the saying, "use it or lose it," is true when it comes to the human body as well.

Maintaining a strong connection to family and

friends plays a huge role in aging gracefully. In many cultures, elders are revered for their wisdom and knowledge—and treated with utmost respect. This has a powerful effect on longevity by increasing a sense of belonging, fulfillment, and happiness. Statistics show that older people living in isolation, who never have family or friends to visit them, are not as healthy and vibrant as those seniors with close relationships. They die much sooner—and far less happy!

Having a sense of humor also helps us age gracefully. People who can't laugh at themselves or find humor in the human condition won't live as long as those with "light hearts." Now scientists are telling us why. Laughter releases a flood of endorphins in the brain, lowers the blood pressure, and relieves stress. It's simply good for the soul.

Having a purpose in life and being directed *outwardly* promotes long life, happiness, and fulfillment. An interesting phenomenon occurs when we do this: By being focused on others' needs before our own, we ourselves also benefit from that selflessness. Doctor Viktor Frankl, author of the wonderful book, *Man's Search for Meaning*, would call this "transcendence," going beyond our own selfish interests for the sake of others. To Frankl, this is the highest state of human fulfillment.

I think a lot of aging gracefully has to do with letting go. When we cling to the things of this world such as money, youth, power, prestige, and material possessions, we lose sight of what's important and why we are here. God tries to remind us, "Remember, Man, thou art dust, and into dust thou shalt return." We came into the world with nothing; we will leave with nothing. But we keep forgetting that.

Our destiny is not found here on earth; it is something a whole lot better. And it will last forever. When we remember that and the more important things in life—family and friends, service to others, learning, having a sense of humor, staying mentally and physically fit—getting older becomes merely a stepping stone toward our ultimate destination.

Regretting the Past and Worrying about the Future

I think most of us would admit that we spend too much time regretting the past and worrying about the future. Very few of us are able to fully enjoy the *present moment*. Our minds are often "stuck" as we contemplate past mistakes or racing ahead to solve upcoming problems or plan future events. In the meantime, the present rushes by and totally escapes our notice.

But life can only be lived *now*. Like the sands of an hour glass, the grains lying at the bottom cannot be brought back, and the grains above haven't fallen yet. We experience life only in the present as that single grain passing through the center. Sadly, the past and the future often rob us of that unique moment in time.

So how do we remedy this? I think it starts with being more aware of where your mind is *right now*. Are you mentally in the past, the present, or the future? If you're somewhere other than the present, stop and take notice of what is happening around you right now. For example, if you're sitting on a beautiful beach in Cancun checking business voice mails on your cell phone, you're failing to live in—and enjoy!—the present moment.

My sons' baseball games could sometimes be a

bit "slow," so I would often bring a magazine to fill voids in the action. However, when my sons would be in the field or up at the plate, I always put the magazine down and was fully engaged in what they were doing. However, they would tell me later that if they were on the bench waiting for their turn to bat and saw me reading, they got the feeling that I wasn't interested. What I may have thought was a more efficient use of my time was probably a failure to live in the present—at least from my boys' perspective. My two girls said the same thing about their soccer games when I would read during halftime, so I guess I'm guilty as charged.

Failure to fully live in the present moment is regrettable when it makes you miss events that can never be recaptured. Certain opportunities occur once in a lifetime. For example, your kids will only be three-years-old one time. They will eat their first ice cream cone, hit their first home run, or sit on Santa's knee for the first time only once. After that, the opportunity to enjoy those milestones as a parent is gone forever, and that's sad.

Two other thieves of the present are regret and worry. Regretting the past is a total waste of time and energy. We can't go back in time and change *a single thing*. And yet, we will often try. But those sands of the hour glass have already fallen. Focusing on the past only distracts us from giving our best effort in the present. You often see even professional athletes compounding a previous mistake and making another because they couldn't let go of the previous blunder and concentrate on the new task at hand.   But in truth, the *only* thing we can acquire from the past is wisdom, which is a nice way of saying learning from our mistakes.   And worrying about the future only bogs us down with needless anxiety in the present moment. Most of the time, the things we fear never happen anyway. And if they do, they are not as bad as we imagined. It's okay to use the present to plan and prepare for the future, but worrying about it never is.

So, in summary, get in the habit of asking yourself, "What am I missing *right now*, and especially, is it something that can never be recaptured?   Where is my mind—and where should it be? Is this the best use of my time?" With practice, you will get a little better each day at living in the present, the only place where life can really be experienced.

"The First Will Be Last"

Even Jesus of Nazareth had to deal with those seeking special privileges. He was once confronted by two of His apostles, James and John, who entreated Him to give them the positions of honor and prestige at His right and His left when He went into His kingdom. Jesus merely counseled James and John, "If you wish to be great, seek the position of servitude first."

We always seem to be battling this selfish side of our human nature, "looking out for number one." I don't know that we can ever cure this tendency, even in a lifetime. At best, we can only lessen it.

What brings out this negative trait that we all share? I think it starts with comparing ourselves to others. As soon as we do that, we become aware of a pecking order and our place in it. If we're not number one, we *want* to be.

But whether we've achieved that status or not, there are negative consequences for all who play the comparison game. The person who is "top dog" often becomes arrogant and defends his position at all costs. Everyone else is seen as a threat, so he hoards power, knowledge, and status. But in doing that, he becomes isolated, and therefore alone, cut off from the joy of human camaraderie. Taken to extreme, this can turn into the megalomania and paranoia of an Adolf Hitler or a Josef Stalin.

For those climbing the ladder, moving up becomes an obsession, and they will do whatever it takes to get there, ethical or not. They too become isolated and lonely because everyone else is seen as a competitor, not to be trusted. Neither the top dog nor those striving for that position are willing to share their secrets with others. They fail to experience the joy of collaboration. They find no sense of teamwork and camaraderie in the pursuit of a shared goal.

I suppose if we could reflect on the sad consequences that result from this constant battle to be number one, we wouldn't find it so alluring. We would be able to find contentment in an honest effort to achieve something worthwhile *as part of a team*, with no concern over who gets the credit. The painful price of our arrogance and envy is the loss of joy and camaraderie. It also creates long term stress on our bodies, minds, and souls. And in the end, we should remember that in God's eyes, it won't matter anyway because "the first will be last, and the last first."

The Power of Gratitude

"Thanks!" It's such a simple word, but it can have enormous impact on another human being. And yet, we often forget to use it. Why? Perhaps it's because we take people for granted. Their daily impact on our lives becomes ordinary, routine—and unappreciated!

The bus driver who picks us up every morning at the corner and drops us off at work while we sit back and read the newspaper, listen to our iPods, or catch a few more winks escapes our notice. He's as regular as clockwork and probably started his own day hours before our own alarm clocks went off. But do we ever say, "Good morning," or even acknowledge his existence? It's not until there's a bus strike that we become painfully aware how valuable his service is.

Or maybe it's the cleaning lady at the office, who empties the wastebaskets and scrubs the sinks, who's invisible to us—that is, until she calls in sick and there are no paper towels in the washroom and the dust is thick on our desks.

There are thousands of people who contribute to our daily lives, most anonymously and without fanfare. They are easily forgotten. But a kind word or a "thank you" would catch them totally by surprise and make their day. One of the great joys in life is seeing the positive impact we can have on another human being, to watch their faces light up with a smile due to something we said. Even just a friendly greeting can work wonders.

One of the most important gifts we can give to another person is to let them know they matter, that they are loved and appreciated. This applies not only to close family members but to perfect strangers as well. In fact, the impact on someone *we don't even know* can be far greater because it's totally unexpected.

There is no way we can touch the lives and show appreciation to all the people who cross our paths every day, but each of us can do a little bit better than we did yesterday. That small extra effort could have enormous impact on our families, our communities, and the world.

Tapping into the Wisdom
of Seniors

When I was young, I spent my summers at my grandmother's old Victorian cottage on northern Lake Michigan. We would spend hours sitting at the kitchen table savoring her lovingly-brewed Maxwell House coffee, talking about anything and everything. I always enjoyed her light-hearted sense of humor—probably the reason she never got "old." She was my link to the family's past, and I cherished her stories about relatives, whether they were the "black sheep," the eccentrics, or just "normal folk." Her wisdom and insights about relationships, politics, and just about anything always amazed me. I began to appreciate the treasured resource she was, a wonderful sounding board for any idea I might have. I will always miss her, but I am not sad because I hope to see her again someday in an even better place.

Now that I am older—and one generation closer to fulfilling the same role as my grandmother—I wonder if we still appreciate what our oldest family members can teach us. Will their wisdom be lost as they are "put out to pasture"?

In generations past, this country was much more connected to older family members. We had a greater appreciation for what they had to offer. In this regard,

I think Americans can learn a lot from other cultures of the world who still cherish and respect their oldest family members. They don't cast them aside simply because they may be *physically* less capable. *Mentally and spiritually*, our grandparents—and oldest citizens—usually have much more *depth* than we do, and this makes them a great resource for us. Sadly, their wisdom often goes untapped.

However, we're now seeing some encouraging signs that this "Greatest Generation" is regaining the importance they deserve. After all, these are the survivors of the Great Depression who overthrew Fascism in The Second World War, preserving our democratic way of life. As thousands of veterans pass away each day, we are trying to interview as many as we can before their oral histories are lost forever. Much of this effort was the result of the dedication of the World War II Memorial on the Mall in Washington, D.C.

Typically, members of the Greatest Generation tend to downplay their role in history. They will tell you that they were "simply doing their duty." They are universally humble and will only tell their inspirational stories *if asked*. Even then, they will claim that it "wasn't anything special." But it *was* special. Furthermore, aside from the historical perspective they can give us, they have a wealth of wisdom to impart. But once again, we must value what they have to offer *and ask*.

It's not too late to bring respect for our elders back

into the American culture. It happens one family at a time. Each of us knows older family members who've been neglected, their wisdom untapped. Start today by reaching out to them. What they can teach will astound you!

Boredom

Life is like a beautiful symphony. The silence between the notes is just as important as the notes themselves. Great composers knew this. Striking notes without a pause in between is just noise, not music. So what makes *us* believe that we must always be stimulated, on a continual high?

I think sometimes it's because empty moments make us feel restless and bored. We have the compulsive need to *always be doing something*. Otherwise, we feel unproductive, like we're wasting time.

But people need time for reflection and growth. Periods of silence and calm allow us to do this. In fact, they are so important that they may need to be *scheduled* in the lives of busy people. Even Our Lord made time to steal away and connect with His Heavenly Father in a night of prayer. People's demands on His time were unrelenting, but He needed these quiet moments to refresh His spirit. If Jesus himself saw the importance of reflection and meditation, shouldn't we?

These quiet times also give birth to our "Eureka moments." Ideas that may have been fermenting in depths of our subconscious minds may now bubble to the surface. Or perhaps we simply use these periods of silence to be in communion with Almighty

God, a great opportunity to thank Him for His many blessings, ask for His guidance in our lives, or simply listen for His quiet messages.

I doubt that we ever have original thoughts. Rather, I think ideas come to us when we tap into the universal mind of God. If we use these periods of "boredom" to connect with Him, we'll be amazed at the ideas He plants in our minds and the effect He can have in our lives.

Balance

Remember that you are body, mind, and spirit. All of these must be nourished. Neglect any one area, and the others suffer.

The bodily dimension is easy to understand. Eat the right foods and get enough rest and exercise. Challenge yourself physically, but don't overdo it. If you get injured, allow enough time to heal.

We also need mental stimulation. This may come through reading, doing crossword puzzles and brainteasers, writing our thoughts in a journal, watching educational TV (while making sure to avoid the mindless drivel that too often passes for entertainment).

Taking care of the spirit is not as easily defined. It involves such things as humor and laughter, the enjoyment of music and art, meditation, watching a sunset, listening to waves breaking on a secluded beach, religious worship, service to others, connecting with friends and family. Often a favorite physical activity can have a spiritual dimension as well: snow skiing through deep powder, surfing the perfect wave, or kayaking down a scenic river.

Do you take care of your body, mind, *and* spirit? Are you overlooking any of these dimensions? Do you make time on your schedule for regular exercise, family and friends, quiet reflection, reading, and recreation? Do you realize that they are just as important to your well-being and success? Or do you focus only on your job at work, to the exclusion of everything else? Unless we recognize and nourish all three dimensions, we will be out of balance and incomplete as human beings.

Be Kind to Yourself and Others

If we took a moment to listen to the things we say to ourselves, we might be appalled at how negative those comments can be. The old saying is true, "We're our own worst critics." Consider that first self-appraisal upon seeing ourselves in the bathroom mirror each morning. It's a good thing we aren't tape recording those words!

And yet, we really *are*, because those negative thoughts, whether they be spoken or not, are recorded *in our minds*. With daily repetition, they become part of our belief system, indelibly etched in our brains. All the more reason to heed the words, "Be careful what you say when you talk to yourself."

If we were to examine the heavy steel cables used in the construction of a suspension bridge, we would see that each cable is composed of many intertwining ropes, and that each rope has many wires, and that each wire has many strands, and finally, that each strand has many fine filaments. The strength of that huge, thick cable, often a foot or more in diameter, is based on the strength of its components, laid down one tiny filament at a time.

Our habits, good or bad, are laid down in much the same way, one filament at a time. Is it any wonder that it takes so long to correct a bad habit! Over hours, days, months, and years, we reinforced it until it became the strongest of cables, difficult to break. So why should we expect to unravel it *overnight*? And yet, we become highly self-critical when we're not able to achieve *instant improvement*. It is much more rational to believe that it will take as much time to break a bad habit as it did to create it.

Perhaps the lesson for us all is to "lighten up." Don't be so hard on ourselves or others. Remember the words of Frank Outlaw, "Watch your thoughts, for they become your words; watch your words, for they become your actions; watch your actions, for they become your habits; watch your habits, for they become your character; watch your character, for it becomes your destiny."

We must learn to be patient with ourselves and others, for we are all human and prone to making mistakes. After all, only one perfect Man ever walked the face of the earth. And be careful with words; they can tear down more easily than they build up. Be willing to forgive ourselves and others. And remember, even after a lifetime, we will never fully become the person we want to be, but the effort can bring us closer to that ideal if we keep on trying and never give up.

Laughter, Medicine
for the Soul

We've always known that laughter make us feel good, but until recently, we didn't really know why. Now scientists tell us that laughter releases a flood of endorphins into our brains and also boosts the immune system. I'm sure that even more healthful benefits will be discovered over time as scientists explore its effects.

I'm also convinced that laughter is good medicine for the *soul*. Abraham Lincoln, inclined to bouts of depression throughout his life, said it always lifted his spirits, especially during the darkest days of the Civil War when casualty figures from the front were particularly grim. He often remarked that he could not have survived without the tonic relief of humor and laughter. Throughout his life, Lincoln used his quick wit and humorous stories to illustrate a point, amuse his friends, or relieve tense situations. In the process, he became one of our most beloved leaders.

Famous author, Norman Cousins, prescribed a large dose of humor for himself as he fought terminal cancer. Every day in his hospital bed he watched old Laurel and Hardy and Charlie Chaplin movies and read every humorous book he could get his hands on. While the doctors were skeptical at first that Cousins's unusual regimen would do any good, they were amazed to see his cancer go into remission.

Humor has been used many times throughout our history when men have faced daunting situations. During the Cuban Missile Crisis, Kennedy and his advisers used it to maintain their equilibrium as they faced the possibility of nuclear annihilation during those frightening days of October, 1962. The Founding Fathers employed gallows humor in 1776 as they put their signatures on the Declaration of Independence, "If we don't hang together, then surely they will hang us separately."

Humor has an amazing ability to defuse tense situations and spread oil on the waters during tough negotiations. It serves as a pressure relief valve when emotions run high. I'm sure the Good Lord Himself had a quick wit and a wonderful sense of humor. Who better than He understood the folly of the human condition! After all, He created us and knows us better than we know ourselves. I think He gave us humor to deal with the low points in our lives. Like Himself, it provides perpetual sunshine during our darkest days.

What is "Success"?

What is "success"? Many would say it is measured by great wealth. Others might say it is how much prestige, power, and influence you have, or the ability to strike fear into the hearts of other men. Perhaps it's fame, good looks, or the ability to attract the opposite sex. Or it might be great athletic achievement, musical virtuosity, winning an Oscar, the Nobel Prize, or a Pulitzer.

But is *great achievement* a necessary ingredient for success? Helen Keller once said, "I long to accomplish great and noble tasks, but it is my chief duty to accomplish humble tasks as though they were great and noble. The world is moved along, not only by the mighty shoves of its heroes, but also by the aggregate of the tiny pushes of each honest worker."

Perhaps that's the secret. We don't have to be like Donald Trump—with a succession of "trophy wives," a gazillion dollars, and multiple buildings and casinos with our names prominently displayed on them in twenty-foot-high letters—to be a success. Rather, we can emulate women like Mother Teresa who achieved true success by her impact on the poor and downtrodden of the world. She had nothing in her bank account, wasn't the president of any nation, and yet was more "successful" than Donald Trump will ever be.

We are all given certain gifts and talents—some more, some less. I think success is measured by how well we use them, but even more important, *how we use them for the benefit of others*. In the end, we will be measured by one simple standard, "To whom much is given, much will be expected." The question won't be, "Did we make history?" but rather, "Did we make a difference to our fellow man?"

What Will Your Epitaph Say?

Stephen Covey, in his book, *The Seven Habits of Highly Effective People*, tells us to "begin with the end in mind." Just as an architect would never think to start a building without a set of blueprints, neither should we live our lives without a vision of what we want to become. And a life is far more important than a concrete edifice!

One technique that might serve us well is to think ahead and consider how we'd like our epitaph to read. What would someone say giving our eulogy? Ebenezer Scrooge, in Charles Dickens's *A Christmas Carol*, faced that very thing when the Ghost of Christmas Future showed him how people spoke of him at his funeral. It was none too flattering and made him completely change the way he led his life. Alfred Nobel decided he wanted to be remembered for more than just his invention of dynamite.

In other words, we should *live our lives backwards*. Decide what we want to become—what our tombstones will say—and then do the things in life that will bring that about. That may be the best way to ensure a life well lived.

Understanding the Power of Forgiveness

We often look at forgiveness—which, in itself, is hard enough—as something we do for other people. But if you examine it more closely, forgiveness is also something we do for ourselves. Remembering slights, holding grudges, and seeking revenge is like acid, eating away its container. If we hold anger inside, it damages us. And the longer we hold on to it, the more damage it does, physically, mentally, and spiritually.

Forgiveness is liberating, both asking for it and granting it. When we ask others to forgive us, it allows us to let go of the guilt for past transgressions. This holds true, whether they choose to forgive us or not. When we forgive others, it doesn't mean that we've forgotten what they did, just that we're not going to let it poison us anymore. The Lord's Prayer says, "Forgive us our trespasses, as we forgive those who trespass against us." A frightening double-edged sword, isn't it? It asks us to examine our own ability to forgive others, because that's the standard that will be applied to us. George Herbert tells us, "He who cannot forgive breaks the bridge over which he himself must cross."

How well are you able to ask for and grant forgiveness? Are you aware that holding grudges and harboring thoughts of revenge damages your spirit? Viewed in that light, does hurting yourself even make sense?

Aim High, But Don't Fear Failure

Aim high, but don't be afraid to fall short. However, more often than not, the fear of failure prevents us from attempting our best effort. In fact, many of us might admit that we aim a little bit low so that we have a better chance of succeeding, for who wants to risk humiliation or become a laughingstock!

But this is not living life to its fullest. Great achievements have always been a "stretch." Where's the joy in mediocrity? There is none! Rather, I like what Teddy Roosevelt once said:

> It is not the critic who counts, not the man who points out how the strong man stumbled or where the doer of deeds could have done better. The credit belongs to the man who is actually in the arena; whose face is marred by dust and sweat and blood…and who at worst, if he fails, at least fails while doing greatly, so that his place will never be with those timid souls who know neither victory nor defeat.

The fear of failure frequently paralyzes us, and yet it shouldn't, for even the greatest men and women of history failed, often *many* times. Look at Abraham Lincoln. His life was a string of failures.

He failed in business, failed to get reelected to the House of Representatives, failed to win a Senate seat, had a troubled marriage, and suffered from severe depression to the point that his closest friends thought he would commit suicide. And yet, in spite of all that, Lincoln is regarded by historians as our greatest president and is universally loved by all Americans.

Watch basketball teams who try to protect a lead near the end of a game. They stop playing in the way that got them ahead in the first place, and instead, take on a defensive posture. As their opponents continue to whittle away at their lead, their body language changes dramatically. They frequently look up at the scoreboard or toward their coach on the bench with pained or helpless expressions. They start complaining about every officiating call, expecting the refs—or someone—to bail them out. They are extremely tight. All of their shots start clanking off the rim. Their goal has switched from *winning* to *not losing*. Of course, that's the death knell in competitive sports. Unable to regain their offensive rhythm, "the wheels come off" and they can do nothing but watch their opponents surge past them. We've all witnessed this scenario and know that it happens.

Heavyweight boxer, Jack Dempsey, had the right attitude. He was once asked why he agreed to risk his championship by climbing into the ring with a tough opponent. He replied that it was no longer *his* championship anyway once he signed the contract to fight. From that point on, it was either man's to win. A true champion doesn't fear losing. Rather, he focuses on winning. That's why they say, "A coward dies a thousand deaths, a brave man dies but one."

Babe Ruth was one of the greatest home run hitters in baseball history. To see him swing at a pitch gave true meaning to the words, "Swing for the fences." Babe held nothing back. While hitting all those home runs, he also led the league in strikeouts, but that never discouraged him. He wasn't afraid of failure. He was never tentative at the plate, for he knew that failure goes hand in hand with great achievement. Are we willing to swing for the fences? Can we commit to our vision and put it all on the line, holding nothing back? Remember, half-hearted efforts usually end in failure.

When we overcome our fear of failure—or at least minimize and control it—we have a better chance of achieving something we can be proud of for the rest of our lives. Perhaps what we accomplish may even leave a legacy that endures long after we're gone. No one ever remembers mediocrity, but true greatness lives on forever.

The Secret to Excellence: Practice and Hard Work

As we watch a pair of figure skaters compete in the Olympic ice dancing competition, we can't help but marvel at the jaw-dropping brilliance of their performance. Their synchronization, their timing, and their athleticism are simply astounding. For the majority of us who have never laced up a pair of skates, it's impossible to appreciate the amount of practice that went into making such beautiful choreography look effortless.

Or perhaps we remember one of Michael Jordan's spin moves as he flew to the basket for one of his signature dunks. We can't help but think that he must have come from another planet, for what we have just witnessed defies the laws of physics. It's hard to imagine that Michael was once cut from his high school basketball team. While that might have made a lesser man quit in disgust, it simply stoked his athletic fire. His practices took on a furious intensity, and we all know the result. He became the standard by which all future basketball players would be measured.

Whenever we see a brilliant performance in any field of human endeavor, be certain that it didn't come easily. Sure, there are rare virtuosos who have gifts that appear once in a generation, but even *they* had to endure hours and hours of practice, over an entire lifetime, to fully develop these gifts. They may make it look easy, but underneath that brilliance is years of hard work.

What does that mean for all of us? Simply, that if we want to achieve anything worthwhile, we must put in the effort and sacrifice required. It's far too easy to dismiss high achievement as the domain *only of the gifted* and to use that as an excuse for not even trying. Sure, they may have a head start, but there is much more to be said for hard work and dedication. In the end, that can make all the difference in the world. We may even surpass those born with so-called *natural gifts*.

Don't Rest on Your Laurels

If you take a snapshot of the top ten companies on the New York Stock Exchange at ten-year intervals over a period of several decades, you discover a most interesting phenomenon: Many of them lost their positions and faded from glory. Several even went bankrupt. What happened? Simply, they stopped doing the things that made them great companies in the first place. They became self-satisfied and complacent. Success became an opiate, and ultimately, led to their undoing.

Isn't it interesting how success can breed arrogance and complacency?

Samuel Tilden tells us:

> Success is a ruthless competitor, for it flatters and nourishes our weaknesses and lulls us into complacency. We bask in the sunshine of accomplishment and lose the spirit of humility, which helps us visualize all the factors that have contributed to our success. We are apt to forget that we are only one of a team, that in unity there is strength and that we are strong only as long as each unit in our organization functions with precision.

Another thing we often hear is, "If it ain't broke,

don't fix it." But it's a huge mistake to make this your philosophy, whether it's in business or life. Why? Because *any* human endeavor can be improved. For example, your company may once have been the greatest manufacturer of buggy whips, but if it failed to see the future impact of Henry Ford's "Tin Lizzy," it was soon out of business.

Later on we saw what happened to the American auto industry in the 1950s, 1960s, and 1970s when their attitude became, "Hey, if we build them, they'll buy them." It took the Japanese, with an interest in discovering *what customers really wanted*, to teach us a valuable lesson in humility. Hubris back then nearly destroyed the American auto industry. And in the last few years, the major U.S. automakers had to fight for their lives once again, some declaring bankruptcy in order to survive.

Resting on your laurels can be the kiss of death, both figuratively *and literally*. It's startling to learn how many executives die soon after they retire—*if they don't find something worthwhile to do with the rest of their lives*. Many times we've heard that "a rolling stone gathers no moss." It's an aphorism that hits home. Human beings must keep moving forward. They can't let their bodies, minds, or spirits atrophy by standing still. If they decide to take a lengthy breather on the bench, they may never get back in the game.

So what keeps us from moving forward? As we said before, often it's complacency, that self-satisfied feeling that "we've arrived," that causes us to stagnate. We think we've achieved everything that needs to be done. It's amusing to think that someone once arrogantly declared that the U.S. Patent Office should be closed, since everything that could be invented, *already had been invented.* It's hard to believe that an intelligent man would express such hubris, but haven't we all fallen into that trap once or twice ourselves? Haven't we all patted ourselves on the back and said, "Well done. Our work is finished here. No one could possibly improve on this!"

Or perhaps we rest on our laurels because we live in mortal fear of losing what we already have. Just like the basketball team we talked about earlier who protected their lead and played tentatively, only to watch helplessly as their advantage slipped away. Before they could stop the slide, it was too late. The momentum had already shifted and their opponents were now a runaway train, impossible to stop. Better to be like Jack Dempsey, who took on all comers and never thought he had permanent ownership of the heavyweight belt. Rather, he had to earn it again every time he stepped into the ring.

Often pride is at the root of our tendency to rest on our laurels. We become so concerned with how others perceive us, that we "play it safe" and avoid attempting new things because they might end in failure and damage our reputations. I wouldn't be surprised if that isn't what sometimes causes a baseball "legend" to retire. Having batted .327 his whole major league career, he can't endure a couple of seasons batting .298, even though that's still quite respectable and would help his team. He's so concerned with his legacy that he is no longer willing to risk failure or look bad in front of his fans.

But often, the greatest kind of courage—and humility!—is the willingness to lay it all on the line even when it risks our reputation. It takes "real guts" to climb down off the pedestal and risk failure by "being in the arena," as Teddy Roosevelt would say. If you're already Number One, the "Champ," or the CEO, you only have one direction to go, and that's down. Why risk it? But that's where true greatness lies: striving to be better, to move forward into uncharted waters even though failure might be the result.

Michael Josephson, a renowned speaker on the subject of ethics, sums it up nicely for us, "What's crucial is to *begin*. Things happen and opportunities appear most often when we're moving, not when we're standing still."

You Matter, and So Does Everyone Else

It's hard to imagine the unlimited powers of an Infinite God who knows us so well that He is able "to count the hairs on our heads." To do that for even one human being would seem impossible, let alone the seven billion who inhabit the earth. And yet, that's exactly what He's able to do, for there are no limitations or constraints on Almighty God.

At the same time, it's utterly astounding to think that He wants a *personal relationship* with every single one of us because we are *that* important to Him. While we often lose track of our own relatives, a number which for most of us is less than 100 individuals, God never loses track of the seven billion humans on earth, even though we may forget *Him* for long periods of time. However, when we need His help, isn't it odd how we suddenly remember that He exists? We are extremely lucky that God isn't that kind of "fair weather friend."

It's also reassuring to know that there is an Infinite Power Who loves us and accepts us to a degree that we can't even comprehend. Sometimes, however, we put human limitations on God's love, assuming that He can't embrace *everyone*. We saw this during the Civil War when churches all over the North and South prayed for victory. We see it today in locker rooms all over the country when each team prays for the win. But it's folly to think that God favors one team over another. Rather, the victory usually goes to the most talented, the most prepared, and the one who works the hardest.

God looks into each of our hearts and knows what lies within. He loves us all but is especially gratified with the return of a "lost sheep." The conversion of one sinner creates greater joy in heaven than the works of a host of saints. When we presume to have the inside track with God, to think that we're somehow better than another person or group, we are sadly mistaken. His love knows no bounds and He plays no favorites. We are *all* important to Him: Christian, Jew, Muslim, man, woman, and child, young and old alike. It is one of the remarkable and wonderful mysteries of God's infinite goodness.

Get Out of Your Comfort Zone

I think we all would admit that we don't like being prodded out of our comfort zones. Once we get into a routine, we prefer to stick with it, especially if it makes us feel secure.

Change does not come easily for us. For example, it might be something as simple as the route we take when we drive to the airport. Rather than try a new way—even though it might save time or avoid traffic—we stick with what we already know. Or perhaps it's an unwillingness to try a new restaurant because we like the old one we've always gone to. After all, we can always order that familiar entrée we've had so often in the past. Besides, there's a risk that the *new* restaurant might not be as good.

Scientists tell us about an interesting phenomenon. If you place a frog in a pan of water and slowly raise the temperature, he will allow himself to be boiled to death before he jumps out. Perhaps we're a lot like that frog, reluctant to tamper with the status quo, avoiding change even if it costs us dearly.

But improvement *always* requires change. In fact, Albert Einstein once said, "The definition of insanity is doing the same thing over and over again and expecting a different result." Change often involves risk, and may even require courage from us. But breakthroughs require bold action and are not for the faint of heart.

When faced with a challenge, we must ask ourselves, *"What's stopping me?"* More often than not, the answer is the fear of failure—or just pure laziness. But look what happened to that boiled frog. He stayed put and ended up dead. We too can be just as dead. Maybe it's not physical death, but the death of our spirits, a far worse fate.

Often we're not even aware that change is happening. But spend an evening looking at old family photos and you'll be able to see that it's a natural part of life. After you've laughed at your old baby pictures, would you really want to remain in diapers for the rest of your life!

We all need to get comfortable with change and be able to embrace it is a requirement for a full and rewarding life. It's the only way to be better today than we were yesterday.

Let Your Talents Guide You

Every one of us has been given certain natural gifts. These talents were bestowed on us by the Good Lord at birth and were certainly nothing we earned through our own merits or efforts.

So how do we discover them? Simply, by being willing to try new things throughout our lives. Eventually we discover what we're good at. Usually they're the things that bring us the greatest joy and satisfaction. Another sign that we're on the right track: When we employ our God-given talents, time seems to fly by without us even being aware of it.

Sometimes a talent rises to the surface later in life. Search your heart. Is there something you've "always been meaning to do" but have put off for one reason or another? Perhaps you think it's too late to start, that you're "too old," but that would be a mistake. I'm reminded of Grandma Moses who learned to paint in her 90s and continued to turn out memorable works of art beyond her 100th birthday. I've had friends who wanted to learn to fly since they were teenagers. But while they may have postponed their dreams, they never gave up on them, and got their pilots' licenses in their 40s and 50s.

Much of the joy and fulfillment we experience in life will come from discovering and then exercising our talents. That happiness will be amplified many times over if we also use these gifts for the benefit of others. At the end of our lives, the Good Lord will ask each of us, "What did you do with the gifts I gave you?" How we answer that question will make all the difference in the world!

Total Control Is a Myth

I'm amazed at how often I fool myself into believing that I am "in control." The truth is, much of what we experience in life is totally beyond our control. If we're honest with ourselves, we all spend far too much time trying to *control the uncontrollable*.

This doesn't mean that we throw up our hands and leave everything to chance, just that we do a better job identifying what we can and can't control. For example, we should do everything within our power to do what we think is right and to follow the dictates of conscience. That's something *within* our control. But in spite of our best efforts, some people will still question our motives and misjudge us. That is something *beyond* our control. We can never hope to control the opinions of others, and yet we still act as if we could change their thinking through a concerted effort on our part.

Don't we lose respect for politicians who put a finger into the wind to see which way it is blowing before taking any action? They try to be "all things to all people," and end up inspiring no one. Their futile pursuit of popularity over substance ties them in a straightjacket and nothing worthwhile ever gets done. Better to be like Abraham Lincoln who made courageous decisions that he knew were right, even though many of them were highly unpopular. "Honest Abe" had control over his decisions but knew he could never control the reaction to them. He forged ahead anyway. And despite being vilified in the press at the time, he is now regarded as our greatest president.

All of us need to recognize what we can control and what we can't. Sometimes there are very few things under our *direct* control. Beyond that, we may have *influence*, but even that influence has its limits and diminishes with distance. Beyond our influence lies the vast majority of the world. For example, can I personally control elections in Pakistan? Hardly! Now if I were the President of the United States, I might have some ability to *influence* them. But even if I had all of his power, I might not make one iota of difference. How about world hunger? Can any of us control it and wipe it out? No, but we *can* alleviate the suffering it causes, even if our influence seems like the smallest of contributions.

"How do you eat an elephant?" The answer: "One bite at a time." That's really the crux of the matter. Just because our span of control won't allow us to do *everything* to solve a problem, doesn't mean we can't at least do *something*. And who knows what can happen after we take that first step? Our parents often told us, "You never know until you try." They were right. *Never underestimate the effect one person acting with courage and decisiveness can have!* Where would we be without Rosa Parks, Mother Teresa, Abraham Lincoln, Charles Lindbergh, or Martin Luther King, Jr.?

We started this discussion by saying "total control is a myth," and that's true. But we also have to be careful not to count ourselves out just because a task seems insurmountable. We need to seek a balance, and I think the "Serenity Prayer" helps us do that:

"Lord, give me the serenity to accept the things I cannot change, the courage to change the things I can, and the wisdom to know the difference."

Trying Too Hard

Ever notice that the harder we try, the less success we seem to have? That's because trying too hard takes us out of life's natural rhythms. Anytime we try to force something, it never works. Furthermore, it makes us more anxious, which disrupts our concentration and makes matters even worse.

There is a natural flow to everything in Nature. When we sense that flow and are in tune with it, things fall naturally into place. Athletes talk about "being in the zone" and "being in the moment," where every move seems effortless. For a tennis player, every ground stroke finds the chalk line; for a basketball player, shots hit nothing but net, regardless of the difficulty; and a golfer feels as if he's putting the ball into a manhole. Everything seems easy and effortless. However, as soon as an athlete starts analyzing it and thinking too much, the magic disappears.

This also applies to personal relationships. People meeting for the first time are trying so hard to make a good first impression that they don't act naturally. Conversation is forced—and terribly uncomfortable. Each one wonders, "Who is this stranger talking for me? I would never say something like that! Where did the *real me* go?" If the relationship survives this awkward beginning, it becomes almost laughable when recalled months later when things have returned to "normal."

So how do we combat this tendency to try too hard and then "blow it"? I think the secret is to not make "success" or "winning" so critical to our enjoyment of the things we do. In other words, if we allow winning at all costs to be our only goal, then there is no joy in the *experience* because we are too worried about the *outcome*.

Invariably, the greatest performances—in any field of human endeavor!—occur when the participants let it "all hang out" and just do their best rather than thinking about the gold medal or looking up at the scoreboard. Freed from the worry of the result, their performance becomes magnificent, natural, and joyous. They find "the zone."

I think Sarah Hughes's performance in the 2002 Olympic figure skating competition epitomizes what we're talking about here. Rather than being tentative, she skated with visible joy and gave us the performance of a lifetime. That she also became the Women's Olympic Figure Skating Champion was just a secondary outcome of the way she approached the competition. She let her free spirited, spontaneous, and joyous skating be reward enough. Whether she won the gold medal or not really didn't matter to her. As a result, her exuberant performance will go down in history and be remembered by all who watched her.

I think we all could agree that our culture has put

too much emphasis on winning and not enough on the joys of *participating*. When we learn to relax and have fun, rather than trying too hard to "win," our lives will be much more fulfilling and happy. It doesn't mean that we won't give our best effort, just that we won't let winning be the only thing that gives us joy.

The Power of Example

When it comes to discussions about leadership, much is said about example. What role does it really play? Simply this: *Leadership is 100 percent example, period!* It is your most powerful leadership tool.

Everything we learn about leadership comes from watching leaders in *action*. Words are far less important. In fact, we really don't care much about what leaders say if their words don't match their actions.

Think back. We get our first cues from our parents. Like dry sponges, we soak up everything we observe about them: their mannerisms, speech patterns, behavior, how they discipline, and so forth. The same is true of our own leadership style. It becomes a composite of what we've learned by watching other leaders. And make no mistake about it, we learn from bad leadership as well as good. Hopefully, we decide never to treat other people the way that poor leaders once treated us.

Leaders often don't realize how closely they are scrutinized. But subordinates pick up on *everything*, and *actions* have the strongest impact. If you don't think this is true, attend a going away party for someone in a leadership position and watch the skits and other humorous parting remarks that are made.

You'll often find a hilarious parody of all the leader's peccadilloes.

No figure in history had more impact than Jesus Christ. This humble Man from a small, conquered nation on the fringes of the Roman Empire came to influence the world like no other. And Jesus taught us in the most powerful way: by His example!

"Learn of me," He said, "because I am meek and humble of heart, and you shall find rest to your souls."

His example was a startling contrast to accepted leadership practices of the time. Mercy—especially to one's enemies!—was unheard of. Gentleness was thought to be a sign of weakness. At that time in human history, instilling fear was the only way to exercise control. Most of the known world lived under the boot of the Imperial Roman Army and the Emperor, Caesar Augustus. Any nations who rose up against the empire were slaughtered without mercy. Brutality was an accepted way of life. Only an elite few lived in luxury—and always at the expense of the vast majority who scratched out a meager existence in unremitting poverty. Jesus chose to come into this world, not as one of the privileged, but as the poorest of the poor, born in a shepherd's cave. He grew up in a small, backwater town called Nazareth, a lowly carpenter's Son. But from these humble origins, the way He lived His life gave an example for the entire world to follow.

Early in His ministry, He taught us to revere

the innocence and openness of children. No matter how tired Jesus was, He always had time for them, telling His disciples, "Do not send them away; let the little children come to Me." He taught His followers, "Unless you are like these children, you shall not enter the Kingdom of Heaven."

Jesus felt so strongly about the power of bad example that He once said, "But who so shall offend one of these little ones which believe in Me, it were better for him that a millstone were hanged about his neck, and that he were drowned in the depth of the sea."

Jesus chose the company of sinners and the down and out. When challenged by the privileged Jewish elite about the company He was keeping, He simply replied, "It is the sick who have need of a doctor, not those who are well."

Jesus taught humility and servant leadership by washing the feet of His disciples before their last meal together. When told of the death of His good friend, Lazarus, His compassion was visible. The shortest sentence in the Bible tells us simply, "Jesus wept."

As we mentioned earlier, Jesus was by no means a pushover. He fearlessly confronted the arrogant and the powerful, calling them "hypocrites and a brood of vipers." He showed righteous indignation when He saw the moneychangers desecrating the holy Temple of Jerusalem, "His Father's house." They scattered like vermin as He upended their tables and chased away this "den of thieves."

But the most important example Jesus gave us was His love. He knew that people were starving for a message of hope in their oppressive lives. He came on earth to tell us the "good news" of a heavenly Father and His infinite love for us. He told the people, "Come to Me all you who are heavily burdened, and I will give you rest."

In fact, Jesus' every action was a demonstration of love. He showed us by His example how to be kind, generous, and forgiving. On the eve of His death, He said to His followers, "Love one another, as I have loved you." Ultimately, Jesus made the supreme gesture of love by dying for us on a cross. "Greater love hath no man than this, that He lay down His life for His friends." His example is unmatched in history and gave hope to all of mankind. It is a brilliant light so powerful that it can never be extinguished.

As a leader, what message are you sending? Are you more concerned with your position and privileges than the welfare of your people? Do you pitch in when they need help, or are you a prima donna? There should be no job beneath your dignity. When people know that, it gives you great power as a leader. Set the example and lead by your actions.

Learn from Great Leaders

Much of what we learn comes from mentoring. We can all look back and remember those marvelous people who had such a powerful influence on our lives. They were our moms and dads, coaches, teachers, grandparents, aunts and uncles, brothers and sisters, and numerous others.

However, we don't have to limit ourselves to those whom we met and knew *personally*. We also have the great leaders of history to teach us, and many of them lived long before we were born. We need merely focus on those character traits we admire, and then look for leaders who exhibited them.

It's no surprise that the leaders who could be characterized as "great" shared many of the same qualities. Selflessness, humility, kindness, vision, intelligence, energy, courage, character, and charisma are some of the traits that come to mind.

Who are your personal favorites? My list would include Jesus Christ, Abraham Lincoln, Mother Teresa, Coach John Wooden, Robert E. Lee, Admiral Nimitz, General Chesty Puller, General Eisenhower, Ronald Reagan, Theodore Roosevelt, Mahatma Gandhi, or Pope John Paul II.

They all had character traits that made them stand out and have an impact on the world they lived in. We need merely to study their lives in order for them to mentor us today. It's simply astounding that these men and women can touch our lives in such a dramatic way long after they have died. They are a remarkable resource for our own improvement if we allow them to be. What is even more amazing is that *we can all assemble our own personal mentoring group*, and then ask them to teach us.

Someday in the future, when the question is asked, "Who had the greatest impact on your life?" perhaps someone in the audience will think of *you*. That's a legacy we can all strive for.

Listening

Public speaking courses abound, but how many of us have ever been to a *listening course*? There are very few. And yet, a good conversation requires both: a speaker and a listener who's paying attention.

Isn't it interesting that we were born with two ears, but one mouth? Maybe that should tell us something about the importance of listening versus speaking. But too often our conversations are *dueling monologues*. We don't even bother to listen as we wait impatiently for our own turn to speak and "enlighten."

Dr. Stephen Covey tells us, "Seek to understand, before being understood." That's good advice. *Listening adds to our store of knowledge; speaking does not*. Listening also sends a powerful message to the person speaking: "I have respect for you and what you are saying." And if we set that example with our own empathetic listening, there's a good chance it will be reciprocated.

How well do you listen? Do you monopolize the conversation because you're the boss? Do you think you're the only one with good ideas? Are you missing good inputs because of your attitude?

As a leader, be the last to speak. That will prevent your opinion from biasing the discussion. More untainted views from others will be voiced that way.

People are more likely to say what's on their minds rather than what they think the boss wants to hear.

Give praise to anyone willing to offer a contrary opinion. They are showing courage and may be saying the exact thing that needs to be heard. Remember, yes men are of no value.

Finally, *we must listen to our hearts*. It is the most important form of listening we will ever do. Our hearts speak in soft, quiet voices, so we need to listen very carefully. They give us the best advice we will ever receive. Sometimes the message will be contrary to the direction we are headed at the time, but a change may be what's needed most, and only our hearts will tell us that. The inner voice of the heart is the best friend we will ever have because it is our direct connection to the Almighty.

Be a Perpetual Learner

Continuous learning should be a lifelong goal. The more we learn, the more we discover how little we really know. This is good because it keeps us humble. In astronomy, for example, the unfolding secrets of the universe inspire awe at the infinite magnitude and splendor of the Creator's work. While a number of our questions about the universe are answered, many more new ones are generated. (It often appears that our *ignorance* is expanding much more rapidly than our knowledge.)

There is always more to learn, and hopefully, someone around to teach us. Leaders must realize their shifting roles: sometimes teachers, sometimes students. Acknowledge the brilliance that exists among subordinates. Everyone else is smarter in some way, often in many ways. The wise leader taps into the expertise of those around him. Feigning knowledge fools no one—except perhaps, the leader, himself—and undermines the respect junior people have for "the boss."

Start with the attitude that everyone has something to teach you. Look for the good in people. Ask them questions. Let them educate you. After all, we were made with two ears and one mouth. Maybe that tells us something about the ratio of listening to speaking!

Many icons of America's great corporations

had their biggest breakthroughs when they finally realized they couldn't do it all by themselves. They had to start relying on the knowledge and expertise of others. By doing that, they empowered them, gave them a stake in their organizations, and lifted them to new levels of achievement.

Take advantage of the great leaders of history. Find out what made them great. Read what they've written. Study their lives. More than likely, if you get to know them well enough, you'll realize how "very human" they were, with warts and all. Even the most courageous were sometimes afraid. They made stupid mistakes but were willing to learn from them. They had all of the human foibles we still battle today, but that's what makes them so real. See how they overcame adversity because every one of them experienced, in their own unique way, the "heat of the forge." Abraham Lincoln, for example, faced his demons of depression and loneliness. But he inspires all who study him. His remarkable life, great humanity, magnificent spirit, and humility uplift us. He is a magnificent role model!

So read a lot. Avoid the mindless TV shows offering neither education, inspiration, nor humor. Fill yourself instead with the great ideas and wisdom of the ages. Your mind will amaze you with the novel connections it can make and the ideas it can generate, but it needs to be fed the right raw material. Make being a perpetual learner a lifelong goal.

Be Your Own Best Friend

Give yourself a daily pep talk. It sure beats the daily stream of self-criticism that we often feed ourselves. In fact, if we closely examine our self-talk, we might be appalled at the demoralizing things we say to ourselves. These words are hardly encouraging, and only beat us down.

When we discover this kind of self-talk polluting our thoughts, say the word, "Stop!" This will help to break the stream of self-deprecating conversation. We are indeed our own worst critics and have probably had this habit for many years. Therefore, don't expect an overnight cure. It takes as much time to undo a habit as to create one. Go easy on yourself. Applaud even the smallest steps in eradicating this negativity. Focus instead on the good you bring into the world every day. Remember, whatever you think of yourself, you're right! Philosophers have said it for generations, "What we think, we become." Be careful with your thoughts!

I like this simple method of building self esteem: Do good works; then *remember* that you did them!

Translate Intent into Action

All the good intentions in the world amount to nothing if we don't translate them into action. The blueprint is not the finished bridge. The outline is not the book. Musical notes on a page remain that way until the orchestra plays or the song is sung.

To one extent or another, we're all procrastinators. We create great plans and have many good intentions, but taking that first step is problematic. Perhaps we're overwhelmed by the magnitude of the undertaking. Or maybe it's because the required action will be unpopular. Often, as much as we hate to admit it, we're just plain lazy.

One of the best ways to shake ourselves from this lethargy is to just *begin*. Take that first step. Do *something*. Just like the philosophers tell us, "The journey of 1000 miles begins with the first step."

Another trick is to break the task down into smaller, intermediate steps. For example, in writing a book, play around with the wording of a few sentences first, until you get a paragraph you like. Turn that paragraph into a few more until you have the semblance of one coherent essay. Those essays can then become a chapter in a book. Repeat the process until you have all the chapters you need to complete your story, whether it is a novel, or a non-fiction book. It's the answer to the question, "How do you eat an elephant?" Simply, "One bite at a time."

Sometimes what's needed most is a "gestation period." Task your subconscious mind with a task you want to accomplish, *and then wait*. Without even being aware of it, our creative minds are busily working on a solution, but that takes time.

Henry Ford gave his engineers the "impossible" task of designing a V-8 engine, even though none had ever existed. But this harnessed the power of their creative minds, and soon they were able to build a prototype. Authors often experience "writer's block," but that just means they are going through another creative gestation period. The words will soon flow again.

To sum it up, we must be patient with ourselves. Envision a goal we want to reach, allow our creative minds to come up with a solution, and then take the necessary steps to translate our intentions into reality.

Silence, Peacefulness, and Quiet

As human beings we seem to abhor a vacuum. Silence, peacefulness, and quiet make us restless. There is a desperate need to fill the void, often with idle chatter and meaningless activity. But as the great composers have always known, the spaces *between* the notes are just as important as the notes themselves. They turn cacophony into beautiful music.

In the hurried pace of our daily lives, we often need to pause and reflect on where we are going and what truly matters. Invariably, we may discover that what we are doing right now isn't important and is really a departure from our own life's goals. To the degree that our actions are disconnected from these goals, *we are wasting our time*. We are not really making "music," just a lot of noise.

We often confuse activity for productivity. But being busy doesn't mean we're necessarily accomplishing anything. In fact, it might be just the opposite: All of our chaotic motion may be keeping us from doing what's really important. For example, is being the head chauffeur for our kids, taking them to soccer, music lessons, summer camp, and the like, really building strong family bonds?

Maybe just "shooting hoops" in the driveway or playing catch with our sons is a better use of our time. Or perhaps, wrestling and tickling your kids on the living room floor before bedtime has a whole lot more meaning. When was the last time we read them a story as they nestled in our arms? Have family dinners disappeared from our daily routine? Do we ever sit down and talk to our kids about what's on their minds?

At work, is everything we do about "billable hours"? Do we leave time for friendships to develop? After all, it is camaraderie that separates winning companies from those that fail. Only friends will go the "extra mile" and provide outstanding service for their customers.

In the spiritual dimension, is our time in church spent only singing hymns, chanting prayers, or listening to noisy sermons? Do we ever just sit quietly alone in a church and hear God whispering to us? Then how are we to know what He wants from us!

If we're honest with ourselves, I think we can all do better at listening to the pauses between the notes. In the silence, peacefulness, and quiet much joy and happiness is found.

Never Ask, "Why Me?"

When bad things happen to us, we're often tempted to ask, "Why me?" Perhaps a better thing to say is, "Why not me?"

None of us was meant to lead a charmed life. Why should any of us expect to go through life unscathed? In fact, when we stumble and fall, or encounter a run of "bad luck," we can grow from the experience. It all depends on our attitude.

Let's face it: Life throws us many curve balls. In fact, death, the final curve ball, is the only way we will all leave this planet. But even death is not an end to our existence or the ultimate calamity. After we die, we are meant to live on forever in a glorified state, united with our Creator. That's hardly a dismal fate, but rather one that should give us great hope for the future.

In the meantime, we can stop whining about every little thing that happens to us as if we're being singled out. *Everyone* suffers setbacks. If anything, we should be grateful for our many blessings. Just look around. People in other parts of the world deal with far more misery and calamity—*in a single day!*—than we will encounter *in a lifetime*.

There's an old saying, "Calm seas do not make good sailors." Life's storms can make us better, toughen us up for the long voyage ahead. But be encouraged: We will ultimately encounter placid waters when our journey has ended.

The Power of Loving Relationships

Adam Smith once said, "We experience true happiness when we feel the love of another human being." Human connections are the source of our greatest joy, second only to the infinite and incomprehensible love our Creator has for each and every one of us.

Those who seek happiness in material possessions are destined to experience disappointment, frustration, and emptiness. Like heroin addicts who must keep increasing the dosage to get the same high, they buy a bigger boat, a faster car, or a more palatial estate only to discover that their pleasure is merely temporary. In a very short time, they are restless again, looking for their next "fix." What once gave them "happiness" has all too quickly lost its allure.

Loving relationships are all that matter. Parents will often work long hours just to bring in larger paychecks so that their children will have material things. But they are missing what their sons and daughters really need most: their time, love, and affection. Sadly, they discover too late that they cannot go back and relive those Halloweens, school plays, soccer games, or birthdays they missed. Kids only grow up once—and seemingly, in the blink of an eye! When parents finally realize that those moments are gone forever, never to be recovered, it's too late. Their children are now adults, remote and distant, and they can't understand how they got that way.

Connecting with another human being, feeling their love and loving them in return, is the only thing that brings true happiness. Nothing else compares: not wealth, not power, not possessions, not prestige or position.

Even life itself comes second to love. In Jesus Christ we see an example of the greatest love of all "that He laid down His life for His friends." That love continues to be the most powerful force in the universe. Apart from it, we cease to exist and become mere dust. Connected to it, there is nothing we can't accomplish.

Doing Little Things Well

Most of the good that's accomplished in this world is done in small increments by millions of people working in total anonymity and with little fanfare. Out of the limelight, they perform their often routine, day-to-day tasks to the best of their ability without much thought to the impact they are having. Parents do loads of laundry, prepare meals, coach soccer teams, and take out the garbage without any thought of a payback or what's in it for them. And yet, it is these small contributions that keep families and communities running smoothly.

We don't need to win the Pulitzer or Nobel Prize, discover a cure for cancer, win a national election, or hit the winning home run in the World Series to have an impact. Most of the good in the world comes from millions of selfless acts that might appear meaningless but actually, in their collective impact, make the world go round.

So when you find yourself wondering, "What good am I doing or what have I accomplished?" know that simply doing your best in anything you attempt contributes mightily to the good work that needs to be done in our world every day.

The Power of Believing

Believe in yourself! Start with the premise that you are already creative by nature. You have a wonderful instrument, the human mind, standing by to do your bidding. It merely waits to be programmed with your visions. Believe the answer already exists. Think of the solution as a phone number that you've only temporarily forgotten. Perhaps this sounds like magic or voodoo. But it can be described only as amazing, and it works! Let me illustrate.

I mentioned earlier about Henry Ford who was convinced that his engineers could build a V-8 engine. At the time, it didn't even exist. His engineers said it was "impossible." So what did Ford do? He simply locked them in a room and told them to design one. In his own mind he already knew it could be done. A few days later, his engineers emerged with a V-8, just as Ford had envisioned. He believed in them, and that was enough to empower them to create it.

In May of 1961, John F. Kennedy startled the nation, and certainly NASA engineers, with a speech proclaiming that the goal of this nation should be to put a man on the moon, and return him safely to earth, before the end of the decade. No doubt, the jaws of many NASA engineers hit the floor! "Why, we haven't even put a man in space, let alone sent Him to the moon!" they said. But Kennedy's vision rallied the nation and everyone involved with the space program. He challenged them with a goal, created the possibility long before it became a reality, and that's all it took. He made them believers.

The four-minute mile had always been an impossible barrier until Roger Bannister broke it in 1954. Suddenly, once that psychological barrier had been shattered, many more runners were able to run a mile in under four minutes. In reality, the only thing holding back those other runners had been their lack of belief that it could be done.

The human mind is a phenomenal instrument. It will achieve any goal when programmed properly with your creative imagination. If, for example, your goal is to improve foul shooting, it will learn from every shot you miss and every shot you make. What is most interesting, however, is that while you may initially miss many more than you make, the mind pays more attention to its successes than its failures. In other words, it focuses on success and uses failure only as a stepping-stone to achieve a higher success rate. That is why it is foolish to lament our failures. The mind is programmed only to learn from them, then forget them as it homes in on its primary goal: *success*.

Discouragement and Despair

All of us face discouragement and despair at some time during our lives. Even the Good Lord, Himself, cried out on the cross, "My God, My God, why hast Thou forsaken Me!" If *He* can experience these feelings, surely we can as well. It is a natural human response to adversity.

However, what separates the great men and women of history is their response to tough circumstances. It's not how often you fall that counts, but how often you get up again. It's been said that "success is often the last event in a long line of failures." In other words, failure is the price you must pay for success.

It's normal to feel defeated or discouraged when bad things happen to us. But to wallow in self-pity and despair does nothing toward restoring our spirits and self-confidence. So how do we become "unstuck"? Sometimes we just can't do it by ourselves. We must acknowledge our own weakness and call on the Almighty for help. This is actually a sign of strength because it honestly faces the reality that we can't do it on our own, so why shouldn't we avail ourselves of the most Powerful Force in the universe! We would be foolish to pass up His help, especially since He *never* lets us down.

So remember, when faced with adversity, we're never alone. *And it's only failure if we give up.*

"No Man Is an Island"

The poet, John Donne said, "Never ask for whom the bell tolls; it tolls for thee." What did he mean? To understand, we must transport ourselves to England during that time, the sixteenth century.

Back then, nearly everyone lived in rural farming villages. The church was the tallest building in town, and the church bell rang out for all important events. When it tolled, it announced to all the villagers out in their fields that a death had occurred. But rather than asking, "Who died?" John Donne wants us to realize that the death of any villager really means that a part of the village has died as well, since we're all connected in our humanity.

So it is on any team. We rely on each other. A victory for one is a victory for all. As Ben Franklin, one of the signers of the Declaration of Independence, said with gallows humor, "If we don't hang together, then they will surely hang us separately."

As a leader, does your team hang together? Do they feel connected? Or do you treat them like interchangeable parts in a machine, overlooking their shared humanity? While we may cling to the romanticized American folklore of the rugged individual, making it on his own, that's seldom the way it works in real life. Sooner or later we realize that we can't do it all by ourselves. Henry

Ford introduced the idea of the assembly line. But it would remain a mere *idea* without workers to make it happen.

Even athletes who play individual sports like golf and tennis have their coaches, nutritionists, and sports psychologists. All of mankind's greatest achievements were team efforts. When we look more closely, even solo accomplishments most certainly had the early encouragement of parents, coaches, family members, and other mentors. Only when we work together in concert do we reach our full potential as human beings.

The Mystery of Free Will

At one time or another, amidst the daily barrage of genocide, famines, tsunamis, and terrorist attacks, all of us have probably said, "How could God let this happen?" If He is all-powerful, why doesn't He intervene to prevent these catastrophes?

The simple truth is that God gave mankind the gift of free will. By allowing us to make our own decisions, it creates the possibility that we will choose unwisely, picking evil over good. But if we didn't have this chance to pick evil, then by definition, we wouldn't have free will.

God could have easily programmed us to love and worship Him *involuntarily*, without any choice in the matter. However, He didn't want robots, but instead wanted free-thinking human beings.

As our Heavenly Father, I'm sure it saddens Him when His children make poor choices. He takes no joy in watching the suffering and tears they cause. But it was more important to Him that we have the gift of freedom. What we choose to do with it is entirely up to us.

Do we often blame God for our own mistakes? Yes! But when we fully understand the reasoning behind His gift to us, we will come to understand *our own responsibility* for the choices we make.

Looking Back at the Past

George Santayana once said, "Those who cannot learn from history are doomed to repeat it." History provides many lessons, but too often we fail to learn from them. For example, in the 19th Century, Napoleon's army was decimated by the Russian winter, and yet, the Nazi war machine blundered into the same trap in the 20th Century by invading Russia once again, and thousands more soldiers suffered frostbite or died from exposure.

History also shows us that when we fail to confront evil, we invite trouble later on. We can repeat something horrific like the Holocaust with present day genocide in the Sudan, or, on a lesser scale, spoil children who should have been disciplined early on.

While learning from history is a good thing, becoming mired in the past is self-defeating. If we continue to beat ourselves up over past mistakes, we're going nowhere. We end up discouraged and using the same old solutions that didn't work the first time.

History can also be used to give encouragement by showing us how far we've come. Sometimes we don't appreciate the progress we've actually made until we look back and see where we started. Rather than be discouraged, we should see the large, overall leap we have made.

In summary, we should only use history to teach, encourage, or give us perspective, but never to beat ourselves up over past mistakes.

So What? We're Human

So we've made mistakes, looked foolish, and often embarrassed ourselves. So what? We're human. We need to give ourselves a break. Mistakes only have value in what they have to teach us. Nothing more! Beyond that, they only break us down, discourage, and diminish us. Dead ends, doors slamming in our faces, missteps and failures often have only one underlying purpose: to get us moving in a new direction!

Every one of us has had the experience of looking back and seeing the dramatic new direction our lives have taken after a certain path has been blocked. At the time, we were at our wits end and didn't know why it was happening, but later we were glad that it did. Perhaps it was a job that we desperately needed and felt well qualified for but didn't get. Someone else—perhaps less deserving—was hired instead. Later, however, a new position opened up in an altogether different field and became our life's work. Maybe it was a relationship that seemed perfect, but then didn't work out. But later we ended up marrying the ideal companion, someone who just happened into our lives. It often takes the passage of time to give us enough perspective to see that dramatic crossroads in a new light.

For all of us, the hardest thing to do is to "let go and let God." We're dumbfounded at the curve balls life throws at us, and sometimes, just want to give up altogether. But it is in our darkest moments that we have to trust God the most.

It's hard for us to believe that He has a unique plan for each of us—but He will only act if we get out of the way and let Him do His work. Always remember, God gave us free will, so unless we give Him permission to take over our lives, He won't interfere. We must *invite* Him in, with faith and confidence that no matter how bad things are, He will lead us in the right direction.

Even Jesus, God's beloved Son, facing the horrifying torture and crucifixion that awaited him, cried out in His human anguish, "Father, if it be Your will, let this cup pass from Me." But in the end, He totally surrendered to the Father, "Not My will, but Thine be done." Once again, fully human like us, He set the example for us to follow in our own adversity.

So we basically have two choices in our lives: go it alone or allow our loving God to guide us. He only awaits our invitation. One thing for certain, His outcome will be far better than anything we could achieve on our own.

Our Capacity for Good and Evil

Too often we look at other people and condemn them for their faults, saying to ourselves, "I could never do something as bad as that." But in truth, whether we want to believe it or not, the same capacity for good and evil exists in all of us.

We look at the horrors of the holocaust and wonder, how could the German people allow such evil to exist in their midst, and not react with outrage and revulsion? Perhaps, the story of the boiled frog gives us some insights. It tells us how his water is slowly heated, in very small increments, until, before he realizes it, it's too late to leap from the pot. In much the same way, we humans can slowly become inured to the evil around us, doing nothing, until it becomes an accepted part of the way we live.

Lynchings were common in the Deep South for many decades. Blacks could be murdered for no reason at all, other than the color of their skin. Sadly, we see actual historical photos of whites from an entire town gathered at a lynching as if it were a picnic or a county fair. These men and women were supposedly upstanding, church-going people who saw nothing wrong with treating another human being like an animal to be slaughtered.

We also see the 1950s photos of the forced integration of our public schools, in which whites, their faces contorted in rage, scream angry epithets at young black students walking up the steps to formerly all-white schools. Without the protection of the National Guard, they surely would have been murdered as well.

Looking back at these events, we now wonder what possessed people to act this way? How could black churches be bombed and innocent children murdered? How could peaceful demonstrations be broken up with billy clubs, fire hoses, and German Shepherds? How could peaceful "Freedom Marchers" end up bludgeoned to death and tossed into the nearest swamp? It simply boggles the mind.

But children must be *taught* to hate; they certainly don't come by it naturally. Like the boiled frog mentioned earlier, it's an insidious, gradual process. It might start early with children being told racial jokes by adults who see no harm in a good laugh, even if it's at someone else's expense. The example from adult role models, especially if they are parents, is a powerful influence on these young minds.

Over time, they begin to see other races or ethnic groups as somehow less human, easy to ridicule without any feelings of guilt. Their false sense of superiority allows them to look down on anyone who isn't "like them." At that stage, it isn't long before "lesser groups" have no rights at all. Their property can be seized, they can be herded into ghettos, beaten, and murdered. Meanwhile, a legal system designed to protect only those who are "ethnically pure," turns a blind eye to all of it.

So how do we prevent this from happening again? First, we have to be aware that human beings have this capacity for great evil or great good—and it exists in all of us! How we are taught from early childhood on is critical. We have to be on guard against anything that serves as a bad example and must recognize its potential to do egregious harm. Perhaps the best guidance for us all is contained in these wise words. "Evil triumphs when good men do nothing."

Your Words and Example May Ripple through Time

Not only can your words and example have a powerful impact in the present, but they can ripple through time, influencing future generations. For example, none of us has ever met Abraham Lincoln. And yet his words and example live on and continue to inspire us.

The Great Emancipator was confident and humble enough to pick advisers who were more knowledgeable than he was. And even more important, he was willing to listen to them. He didn't have to be the smartest man in the room and knew when to be the student, and when to be the teacher. By sharing the limelight, he showed his confidence.

In His inaugural speeches, Lincoln always used a conciliatory tone. In fact, every president who has ever used Lincoln as an example has been mentored by one of the greatest role models of all time. "What would Lincoln do?" is always a good question to ask when faced with a tough problem.

John Wooden, the great Hall of Fame player and coach, taught far more than basketball skills. *He taught life skills*. This leader and mentor lives on in the hearts of collegians who played for him. They would be the first to tell you that his teachings continue to influence them in their daily lives, long after their playing days were over. They in turn keep Coach Wooden's philosophies alive as they teach new generations what he taught them.

John Wooden's "Pyramid of Success" has been the theme of many of his books. Those who have had the honor of meeting and knowing Coach Wooden and learning from his example feel blessed, but thousands more who read his books can also get in touch with the essence of this great man. It's no wonder he is considered a "national treasure."

The great men and women of history live on through countless generations. Who among us has not been inspired by the 300 Spartans, Helen Keller, Leonardo DaVinci, Michelangelo, Socrates, Plato, Aristotle, Beethoven, Mozart, Isaac Newton, George Washington, Martin Luther King, Lou Gehrig, Jesse Owens, Thomas Edison, and many more? And who can overlook Jesus Christ, Our Lord and Savior! His influence has had more impact than any other human being who walked the face of the earth.

Truly, "No man is an island." We can decide to be positively engaged in the human race and leave a legacy that will live on long after we're gone, or do nothing and have no impact whatsoever. The choice is ours.

Dust in the Wind

There is a wonderful purpose for our existence, but it cannot be fulfilled without a strong connection to Almighty God. Disconnected from Him, we are nothing more than dust. But in concert with Him, we can achieve the greatness He intended for each of us. To be sure, we often stumble. We can be weak, proud, arrogant, cruel, lazy, and unfeeling. But we can also be generous, strong, selfless, creative, kind, and loving. We only rise to our best selves when we seek God's help. Apart from Him, we are lost.

In these pages we have examined what it means to be human. We have looked at our triumphs and tragedies, successes and failures, and our capacity for good and evil. One thing becomes abundantly clear and bears repeating: *When we separate ourselves from our loving God, we fail miserably!*

Cut off from our Source, we are but dust in the wind. But when God's heavenly breath falls upon that dust, just like Adam, we come alive. His love surrounds us and enables us, and there are no limits to what we can do with the gifts He has bestowed on us!

Appendix
Guiding Principles

Every leader, like the mariners of old, needs stars to steer by. Every action and every decision must be based on these Guiding Principles.

What are your Guiding Principles? What do you stand for? Have you written them down where you can see them and review them often? Do they guide all of your actions and decisions?

You won't always measure up to your Guiding Principles, but they are there to help you get back on course.

Everyone needs to create his or her own Guiding Principles, but as an example, the next page shows the eleven stars I steer by, designed for display on a single page.

GUIDING PRINCIPLES

- Continually develop own character traits to be able to inspire others. Set the example.

- See failure for what it really is: a great chance for growth and learning.

- Lift up everyone you meet.

- Never overlook the value of a sense of humor.

- Learn from everyone you meet.

- Use stories and analogies to communicate.

- Take time to reflect.

- Listen.

- "To thine own self be true..."

- Don't be afraid to say, "I'm sorry," or, "I was wrong." You're human.

- Have the courage to follow God's plan for you.

Here is a more detailed explanation of what those Guiding Principles mean:

1. **Continually develop own character traits to be able to inspire others. Set the example.** You are always a "work in progress" trying to make small improvements every day. And nothing is more important for you as a leader than setting the example.

2. **See failure for what it really is: a great chance for growth and learning.** Use mistakes as stepping stones to ultimate success. None of mankind's greatest achievements was ever realized without a lot of mistakes being made along the way.

3. **Lift up everyone you meet.** Everyone who encounters you should be better off for the experience.

4. **Never overlook the value of a sense of humor.** The ability to laugh at yourself and your own mistakes is critical to your team's success. Humor has the power to defuse the most difficult situations.

5. **Learn from everyone you meet.** Every person you meet is smarter than you are in some way, often in many ways. Know when to be a teacher and when to be a student. It keeps you humble.

6. **Use stories and analogies to communicate.** Many of our best leaders were great story tellers. Don't overlook this great way to communicate.

7. **Take time to reflect.** Pause each day to unwind and reflect on your Guiding Principles and the goals of your team.

8. **Listen.** The Good Lord gave us two ears and one mouth. Maybe that should tell us something about the ratio of listening to speaking. Stephen Covey tells us that an empathetic listener "seeks to understand before being understood."

9. **"To thine own self be true..."** Shakespeare said it best. If you are true to yourself, you can't be false to any man.

10. **Don't be afraid to say, "I'm sorry," or, "I was wrong." You're human.** You're going to make mistakes because you're human. Be ready to make a sincere apology.

11. **Have the courage to follow God's plan for you.** God has a plan for each and every one of us. Have the courage to follow it.

Your Guiding Principles can also help you create your own "Leadership Philosophy." It's important that you communicate this to your team early and often. They need to know what you stand for—and won't stand for! Mine starts on the next page.

Leadership Philosophy

I will follow the Golden Rule and always treat others the way I wish to be treated. I will treat others with the dignity, decency, and respect they deserve as fellow human beings.

I will follow my conscience and always strive to do what is right, regardless of the consequences or the personal price I may have to pay. I will always lead others with fairness and consistency.

I will be a Servant Leader, always putting others before myself.

I will lead others by my example, always trying to give my best effort in anything I do. I will continually develop my own character in order to inspire others.

I will see failure for what it really is: a great chance for growth and learning. I will use mistakes only to teach myself and others, never for self-criticism, regret, or worry.

I will lift up everyone I meet. I want anyone who meets me to be better off for the experience. I will empower others to achieve their full potential.

I will maintain my sense of humor and use it to defuse tense or stressful situations. I will retain the ability to laugh at myself.

I will value growth and learning and remember that everyone I meet has something to teach me.

I will use stories and analogies to communicate, knowing that this is the way the great leaders of history have reached others.

I will take time to listen and then reflect on what I have heard without jumping to conclusions.

I will always be true to myself and never lie to myself or others.

I won't be afraid to say, "I'm sorry," or, "I was wrong," because I am human. I will strive to be tolerant of others.

I will have the courage to follow God's plan for me, knowing that His way, not mine, is always better. I will rely on God and remember that great leadership is impossible without His help.

Name Index

A

B

C

D

E

About the Author

Captain Stew Fisher is a cum laude graduate of the U.S. Naval Academy at Annapolis. He retired from the Navy in 1998 after 31 years of service spanning the Vietnam War and Desert Storm.

Captain Fisher led the Navy's first Blackhawk helicopter combat search and rescue squadron in Desert Storm, working with Navy SEAL teams, and later commanded 2000 men and women at Naval Air Stations Pt. Mugu, Lemoore, and China Lake, California. Awards received include the Air Medal, Presidential Unit Citation, Legion of Merit, and the Meritorious Service Medal.

During his long career, he attended the Industrial College of the Armed Forces in Washington, D.C., and served in the Secretary of the Navy's Total Quality Leadership Office. He authored and taught many of the Navy's quality and leadership courses and was a Strategic Planning Instructor/Facilitator.

In his civilian career, Stew has served as an ISO 9000 auditor. He has developed "The Lighthouse: Advanced Leadership Seminar" which explores the secrets of great leaders, past and present.

Stew is also a black belt in the martial art of Aikido and is a certified FAA Flight Instructor in both helicopter and fixed-wing aircraft.

Stew lives in Camarillo, California, and Trenton, Michigan, with his wife, Yolanda. They have seven grown children and one grandchild: Molly, Kelly, Patrick, John, Jason, Renee, Shawn, and Christopher.

Stew teaches a two-day leadership seminar, "The Lighthouse," based on the principles found in his three books and is available for coaching your team. You can contact him at Tqlmstr@aol.com.

Buy more great reads from this author and others by
visiting our online catalog at
http://www.signalmanpublishing.com

Signalman
Publishing

www.ingramcontent.com/pod-product-compliance
Lightning Source LLC
La Vergne TN
LVHW051059080426
835508LV00019B/1968